Your Affectionate Son

Letters from a Civil War Soldier

Enjoy,
Milann Daugherty

Your Affectionate Son

Letters from a Civil War Soldier

Edited by

Milann Ruff Daugherty

WORD ASSOCIATION PUBLISHERS
www.wordassociation.com
1.800.827.7903

Cover photo of pontoon bridge at Bull Run, Va., 1862
courtesy of National Archives, photo no. 111-B-68

Bloody Run postmark on back cover
courtesy of Barbara Miller

Printed in the United States of America.

ISBN: 978-1-59571-683-5
Library of Congress Control Number: 2011929813

Designed and published by

Word Association Publishers
205 Fifth Avenue
Tarentum, Pennsylvania 15084

www.wordassociation.com
1.800.827.7903

Lieutenant James Cleaver

To

James Cleaver and the Pennsylvania Volunteers
of the Thirty-Seventh Regiment, 8th Reserve, Company F.
They were ordinary men who lived extraordinary lives and
served their nation at a time of deep trouble.

Contents

THE LETTERS 1862

CAMP PIERPONT, LANGLEY, VIRGINIA

CAMP OPPOSITE FREDERICKSBURG, VIRGINIA

CAMP LINCOLN RIGHT WING ARMY

CAMP NEAR BROOK'S STATION, VIRGINIA

THE LETTERS 1863

CARVER HOSPITAL, WASHINGTON, D. C.

PREFACE

The true author of this book is James Cleaver. James was a Pennsylvania volunteer in the Thirty-Seventh Regiment, 8th Reserve, Company F, who served in the Civil War from 1861 to 1864. It is an honor for me to be able to share the letters he wrote during that time. In the year 2011, one hundred fifty years after the beginning of the war, how did this come to be? I'm not positive, but I believe that at some point, my grandmother Anna Cleaver Ruff was given possession of the letters, and she faithfully saved them. After her death in 1959, my grandfather Clay Curtis Ruff continued his wife's vigilant protection of the letters. He brought them with him when he left their home in Slippery Rock, Pennsylvania, to live with his son and my father, Dr. Curtis Cleaver Ruff. Clay Ruff died in 1966, never telling anyone about the letters. They remained unnoticed until 2004, when I happened upon them one afternoon while home visiting. They had been tucked away in the bottom drawer of the dresser in my old bedroom. I was almost speechless when I saw a box full of letters yellowed with age and dated 1861! I was even more intrigued when I saw that the author of the letters was a Civil War soldier and had the last name Cleaver, my grandmother's maiden name.

I'm sure there were times when the letters could have easily become lost or destroyed. But as the letters passed from generation to generation, each guardian must have recognized what a treasure he or she possessed and wanted to preserve this first–hand account of the Civil War. What a journey the letters must have taken as they traveled from 1861 to 2011!

As I began to read the letters, I was overcome with thoughts that I was invading the writer's privacy. James certainly never dreamed that someone three generations later would be reading his letters. And yet I was swept into a relationship with this young writer and felt a true connection that could span the years. I found his letters to be most informative as he spoke about the war, the politics of the day, the issues of slavery and secession, and military life in general. I was inspired as he professed his strong faith in the providence and mercy of the Almighty Father. His expressions of faith revealed how positive he could be in the midst of a war. His attitude reminds us of the difference a true trust in God can make on our perspective.

I found it amazing that James and all the others who served in the Civil War and faced the threat of combat at any moment were still able to exchange letters with their families, and that there were mail carriers who risked their own lives to deliver these letters to soldiers who were constantly on the move.

Two questions came immediately to mind. Did James survive the war and how was he related to me? The answer to the first question is, thankfully, yes. To answer the second question, I began a genealogical search that proved fascinating. Who was this patriotic soldier? James wrote most of the letters to his father, but a few were written to his brother John. To my pleasant surprise, my search was a short one. James's brother John Cleaver was my grandmother Anna Cleaver Ruff's father! James was her uncle and my great-great uncle.

Intrigued by comments made in the letters, I went on to discover that his brother John Cleaver, my great-grandfather, was a Methodist preacher who served from 1858 to 1883. He died in 1884 at the age of 48. Their father, Charles Cleaver, was also a Methodist preacher. This discovery about James's family background helped to explain the strong faith he possessed. Never once in his letters did James ask his father to pray for his safe return. James humbly asked his father to pray only that he remain faithful.

James's letters led me to research what happened to his hometown friends who also served in Company F and to become familiar with other aspects of the Civil War. I am not an expert on the Civil War. My foremost desire is to share James's letters with others who wish to expand their knowledge of that war and to honor the brave men who put themselves in harm's way for what they believed was a righteous cause. The knowledge I have gained appears in italicized text and as Author's Notes accompanying the letters. I believe that this information sheds additional light on James's experiences and enhances his letters.

I hope you will enjoy these heartfelt letters as James allows you to see through his eyes the struggle between the North and South that threatened to divide our country.

ACKNOWLEDGMENTS

Publishing a book is a daunting process. But when you have something that you firmly believe needs to be published, you forge ahead. This book would not have been possible if the letters had not been carefully preserved by our grandparents Clay and Anna (Cleaver) Ruff. I am extremely grateful that they recognized the importance of these precious letters.

I own a huge debt of gratitude to my husband, Bill, who is always supportive of the projects I become involved in. His love and his willingness to be a partner in these endeavors have made them possible. Researching *Your Affectionate Son* meant logging many miles in Pennsylvania. I couldn't have done it without him. In his own words, he is my "wheel man."

I am also grateful to our daughter, Megan Daugherty Ball, for using her talents to create a Web site for the book. Her marketing suggestions have been consistently helpful. (www.uscivilwarletters.com)

I am pleased to include a drawing that was made by our son, Gordon Daugherty, in a junior-high art class. How providential that his rendering of a soldier from the Civil War era would find an appropriate place in this book twenty-five years later. I am so glad I saved the drawing, though I do tend to save everything—a trait I must have inherited from my grandparents.

My parents, Curtis and Roberta (Drake) Ruff, established a home environment conducive to learning. Their wide range of interests was reflected in the enormous quantity of books and magazines in our home. Much of my motivation to compile the letters as a book came from my mother who had a great love of literature and who published a book of her own. Her indelible spirit encouraged me to publish the wonderful letters of James Cleaver.

I wish to acknowledge my brothers and sister and their spouses who share in the excitement of publishing these letters. Their encouragement and interest in the letters are greatly appreciated: John and Holly Ruff; Jim and Adair Ruff; Ken and Lois Ruff; and Marcia Ruff and Tom Wilkinson. John, an artist, and Marcia, a professional editor, lent their expert advice when I needed a little help.

I am extremely grateful to Tom Costello, owner of Word Association Publishers, for reinforcing my belief that the letters were worth publishing and for giving me this opportunity. His help and guidance through the publishing process was professional yet personal.

A book is not ready for others to enjoy until the eyes of a diligent editor have scrutinized every word, comma, and capital letter. For this task, I am indebted to my editor, Nan Newell, from Word Association Publishers. We shared an efficient working relationship as we emailed pages back and forth. Her superb editorial abilities were greatly appreciated, and she made this part of the process a very satisfying and rewarding experience.

Jason Price, also from Word Association Publishers, applied his graphic design expertise to the cover design and formatting of the text and illustrations. It was a privilege to work with both Nan and Jason, and I couldn't be more pleased with the end result.

I appreciate very much the encouragement of those who were interested in reading some of the original letters. I extend grateful thanks to Rev. Raymond Hylton and Abby Sweeney, who were eager to discuss them and share some of their own invaluable insights. Rev. Hylton was also a willing advisor when I needed help with the scriptural references.

I thank those who helped me with my research: Beverly Zona and Chris Fabian at the New Castle Public Library, New Castle, Pennsylvania; and Gillian Kay Leach, Ruth Mackey, and Dr. Raymond Jackson from the Pioneer Library of the Bedford County Historical Society in Pennsylvania. I am indebted to Carolyn Miller Carroll and her mother, Barbara Sponsler Miller, who are two extraordinary historians from Everett, PA. They share my excitement about this book, which honors men from their communities who fought in the Civil War. They generously shared photos and historical information and clarified many questions concerning people who were named in the letters. Their input greatly enhanced the book.

Pen and ink drawing of a soldier by Gordon Daugherty

INTRODUCTION

On June 26, 1860, James Cleaver celebrated his twenty-second birthday. It had been fourteen years since his family emigrated from England to America. He was now a teacher and his whole life lay before him. Before his next birthday, his life and the world as he knew it would drastically change. On April 12, 1861, Fort Sumter was attacked, precipitating the Civil War.

A call went out for volunteers to join the Union Army. James was one of the thousands of young men from Pennsylvania who responded, and he enrolled for three years of service. No one had anticipated the overwhelming response to Lincoln's "call to arms." No preparations had been made with regard to guns, uniforms, or provisions, and there were no training camps. But Pennsylvania did not want to turn away any of these patriotic young men. Since many of these men had signed up for only three months of service, something needed to be done quickly before the North found itself without an army.

It was decided to organize the volunteers into a corps of state "reserves" to be trained in camps around the state. One of these camps was Camp Wilkins, where James and many other volunteers from Western Pennsylvania were sent to carry out their basic training. The camp was located on the site of the old Allegheny County fairgrounds on Penn Street in the Lawrenceville section of Pittsburgh, and was under the command of Col. George Hays, a man of great military knowledge who had commanded a well-known Pittsburgh company called the "Duquesne Greys." It was at Camp Wilkins that the Eighth Reserve Regiment was formally organized on June 28, 1861.

James's Company F was a unit of the Thirty-Seventh Regiment. This regiment consisted of companies that were organized in the Pennsylvania counties of Allegheny, Armstrong, Bedford, Clarion, Fayette, Greene, and Washington. Company F, a Bedford County group of volunteers, was the second to take the field and the first mustered into service for three years. They were known as the Hopewell Rifles under the command of Capt. John Eichelberger and later by his brother Eli Eichelberger. Company F fought from the beginning to near the end of the long conflict. (sources #1, p. 119; #2, p. 756; #3; #58)

As the regiment began to move from one location to another, James continued to write letters home that showed his unwavering commitment to the war effort. In one of his letters he wrote, "I have never regretted the steps I took on the 23rd of April, 1861. I have no doubts about being in the path of duty." [This was the date of his enrollment or enlistment.]

In transcribing all of his letters, which were written over a period of three years, I have generally deferred to James's spelling, capitalization, punctuation, and fondness for underlining. I only used a little editorial license (mostly, adding punctuation or an occasional "sic") when I thought it would clarify the text. I did not want to interrupt the flow of the text, or tamper with his words, which are so eloquent in themselves.

THE LETTERS

—=»«((⦿))»«=—

1861

Bloody Run railroad station where the soldiers bid farewell to their
families and were welcomed home as heroes

Photo courtesy of Barbara Miller

CAMP WILKINS
JUNE 16, 1861

Dear Father,

We have just returned from preaching. In the camp, a young Methodist volunteer of the Middlesex Rangers preach[ed] a very good sermon. He seems to be a young man of talent and very good education. There will be preach[ing] again at 4 o'clock P.M. and prayer meeting in one of the tents at 6.

All is quiet within the encampment. There are no company drills allowed to-day, but there will be a dress parade at 5 o'clock. A company came here day before yesterday from Meadville composed mostly of students from Allegheny College.[1] They are a fine, intelligent-looking set of young men and well behaved, march nicely, and present a pretty appearance.

It does not really seem that men are being trained here for fighting. There is no excitement and no talk about battles and war as there is at Hopewell and Bloody Run.[2] There are 8 companies in camp now and very few disorderly persons among them all. As soon as one misbehaves, he is thrown into the guardhouse. If he attempts it the second time, the usual way is to drum him out of camp after shaving his head and stripping him of his uniform. There have been 2 or three drummed out lately—poor fellows. They looked chapfallen[3] indeed.

One of the members of the Meadville Company has just been here. I stopped writing a while to talk to him. He informed me that their Capt. is a preacher, also some of their other officers. There are in all some six preachers in the company. May God make them and us all useful and instrumental in good. May He bless and preserve our country and its institutions and make us a God-fearing and happy people.

Camp life is not nearly so bad as I expected it would be. We have good food and are comfortable when the nights are warm. Sometimes we are a little chilly at night when they are cool, as we have as yet no blankets.

My love to Mother. I expect to come home in the course of two or three months to see you if we stay here and get our uniforms. Tell Squire Peebles I will write him soon, but at present have a great deal to do.

Write me soon and pray God to keep me faithful. My love to all the people at the Run.

Your Affectionate Son,

Jamie

Author's Notes

James's father, Rev. Charles Cleaver, dedicated the newly built Barndollar Methodist Episcopal Church in Everett, Pennsylvania, in 1860, and continued to minister there for two years.

The following was written by President Lincoln on May 14, 1864, in response to a visit from a Methodist delegation.

"Nobly sustained, as the Government has been, by all the churches, I would utter nothing which might in the least appear invidious against any. Yet without this, it may fairly be said, that the Methodist Episcopal Church, not less devoted than the best, is by its greatest numbers the most important of all. It is no fault in others that the Methodist Church sends more soldiers to the field, more nurses to the hospitals, and more prayers to Heaven than any other." —Edited by Arthur Brooks Lapsley in *The Writings of Abraham Lincoln*, vol. 7, 1906. (source #61, p. 262)

1. The 39th PA Regiment, 10th Reserve, Company I, was largely composed of undergraduates of Allegheny College at Meadville, Pennsylvania. (source #2, p. 813)

2. James was from the Borough of Bloody Run, Bedford County, Pennsylvania, sometimes referred to in his letters as the Run. He mentions many friends from his hometown as well as from nearby Hopewell.

The origin of the unusual name Bloody Run is attributed to an attack by the Delaware and Shawnee Indians on July 5, 1755. The Indians were attempting to stop the shipment of supplies to General Braddock's army at the beginning of the French and Indian War. During the attack, horses and cattle were slaughtered, and it is reported that fourteen men were killed. The stream was dyed red from the blood and the area was known informally as Bloody Run for many years. In 1860 the town officially became the Borough of Bloody Run, a name which lasted less than thirteen years. (source #60)

In 1873 the people of Bloody Run changed the name of their town to Everett in honor of Edward Everett, the orator who spoke at the dedication of the Gettysburg Cemetery just before President Lincoln's address. It is reported that Everett wrote a letter to Lincoln in which he said, "I should be glad if I could flatter myself that I came as near to the central idea of the occasion in two hours as you did in two minutes." Lincoln responded, "In our respective parts yesterday, you could not have been excused to make a short address, nor I a long one." (source # 4, pp. 5, 17)

3. chapfallen, sometimes spelled chopfallen, meaning "dejected or dispirited"; derived from chap or chop meaning "jaw." (source #5)

CAMP WILKINS
JUNE 27, 1861

Dear Father,

Capt. Eichelberger starts for Hopewell to-night. He will remain there until Saturday. Please send my watch. I need it very much. You can send it to Hopewell by mail carrier. Stamps are hard to get here, as we have to go to the post office in the city for them.

All is right in camp. I am busy making out reports for Harrisburg.

My love to all. Try and get out to see us soon. Some are coming from Hopewell on the 4th. Please send my black pantaloons. We have not yet got our uniforms, and I am getting ragged.

I will write to Mother and Lizzie[1] in a few days. Please write soon.

Your Affectionate Son,

Jamie

Author's Notes

Company F soldier: (source #1, p.122; #2, p. 774; #54; #55)

John Eichelberger, Captain, mustered in 6/19/61; captured at Gaines' Mill; wounded at Fredericksburg, Va; discharged by order of War Dept., 3/30/63

1. Lizzie was James's sister, Elizabeth Cleaver (Mrs. John W. Gailey).

CAMP WILKINS
JULY 7, 1861

Dear Mother,

Another Sunday is about to close in camp. Making the fifth of our camp life, and although comparatively quiet, it has been to us the busiest Sunday we have had.

This morning we received our blouses or jackets. Preaching at 9 o'clock by the chaplain of the Regiment, who is of the Presbyterian persuasion and rather a dry stick. After dinner I had to get to work making out the Pay Roll of our Company which was quite a large job, there being three to fill out, each about 26 by 30 inches in size. After that was done I had to march the Company up to Head Quarters to receive our guns. Then came dress parade which lasted until about 6 o'clock. Then supper at 7 o'clock.

After supper, J. H. Williams and I took a walk of about an hour and a half through the suburbs of the city [Pittsburgh] which was delightful indeed. We talked of home and friends, of our present situation and future prospects. When we thought of the chequered[1] stage on which we are acting and of the vanity[2] of every earthly good, the question of "What is life?" forced itself upon us.

We felt that it is truly but as a "span" or a hand's breath"[3] compared with the great future beyond.

Oh, how truly dear to me are these hours of meditation and thought. All the recollections of the past rise vividly before me and the dim misty veil of the future seems at least partly unfolded and I read[4] the end of man. Sometimes painful emotions are awakened, but then in the thought that I am in the hands of and watched over by a kind, wise, and unerring God, there is a solace and pleasure which cannot be defined.

My leisure hours I employ almost entirely in reading, meditation, or in writing.

We have now received our pants, blouses, shoes, and blankets. Expect Monday to receive our caps or hats and on Tuesday our pay. Tell father I got my watch and pants.

Our men all seem contented. We are comfortable and I feel that we are in the line of duty.

May God aid us, bless our cause, and grant us a speedy termination to this civil war. With love to you all, I must bid you good night for Taps[5] have already beat for bed.

Yours Affectionately,

James

Author's Notes

I couldn't help but notice how gentle and philosophical this letter is as he writes to his mother, as compared to all the future letters he writes to his father. He understood the kind of information his mother would want to hear. He shared how he spent his day as well as some of his inner thoughts and wrote a letter that any mother would treasure.

Company F soldier: (source #1. p. 122; #2, p. 774; #54; #55)

John H. Williams, Sergeant, mustered in 6/19/61; mustered out with company 5/24/64

1. British spelling of checkered, meaning "marked by many problems or failures" (source #6)

2. vanity, meaning "worthlessness or futility" (source #6)

   Ecclesiastes 1:2 "All is to no purpose, said the Preacher, all the ways of man are to no purpose" (*Bible of Basic English*);

"Vanity of vanities, saith the Preacher, vanity of vanities; all is vanity." (*King James Version*)

3   Psalm 39: 4-5 "Show me, O Lord, my life's end and the number of my days; let me know how fleeting my life. You have made my days a mere handbreath; the span of my years is as nothing before you. Each man's life is but a breath." (*New International Version*)

4   read, meaning "foretell" (source #6)

5   Usually played on a bugle or trumpet, "Taps" is played today at military burials and memorial services, when lowering the American flag, and to signal the "lights out" command at the end of the day. It concludes all funerals at Arlington National Cemetery and at wreath ceremonies at the Tomb of the Unknown Soldier.

During the Civil War, the U. S. Army Infantry was using the French song "*L'Extinction*" to end the day when Union General Daniel Butterfield decided it was too formal. He remembered a French bugle song called "Tattoo." He and his brigade bugler, Oliver Norton, made some revisions to that song and wrote the melody we use today; however, it was not given the name "Taps" until 1874. It is sometimes known as "Butterfield's Lullaby" or by the lyrics of its second verse, "Day is Done." The popularity of the song spread quickly and was used at a military funeral soon after it was composed. Just ten months after being composed, it was played at the funeral of Maj. Gen. "Stonewall" Jackson. (sources #7, #48) See the Appendix for other Civil War "firsts."

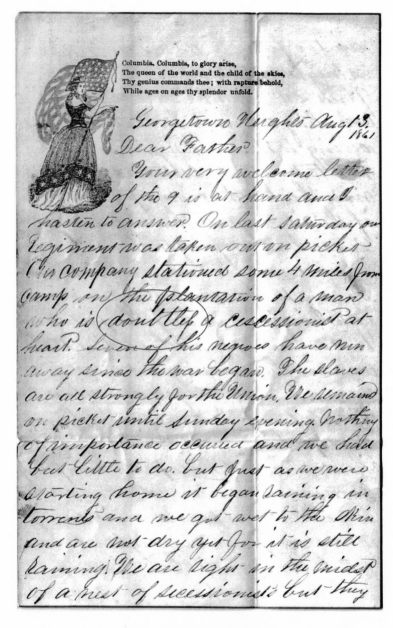

Columbia, Columbia, to glory arise,
The queen of the world and the child of the skies,
Thy genius commands thee; with rapture behold,
While ages on ages thy splendor unfold.

Georgetown Heights Aug 13,
1861

Dear Father

Your very welcome letter of the 9 is at hand and I hasten to answer. On last saturday our regiment was taken out on picket Our company stationed some 4 miles from camp on the plantation of a man who is doubtless a cecessionist at heart. Seven of his negroes have run away since the war began. The slaves are all strongly for the Union. We remain on picket until sunday evening. Nothing of importance occurred and we had but little to do. but just as we were starting home it began raining in torrents and we got wet to the skin and are not dry yet for it is still raining. We are right in the midst of a nest of secessionists but they

James's August 13, 1861 letter
Note the "long S" in "doubtless" (circled)

On the 20ᵗʰ of July, the 8ᵗʰ Pennsylvania Reserve Corps was ordered to proceed to Washington, D. C., by way of Harrisburg and Baltimore where additional equipment was obtained. On July 23ʳᵈ, they encamped at Meridian Hill. They remained there until August 2ⁿᵈ when they moved to the reserve camp at Tennallytown, Maryland. The 8ᵗʰ Reserve encamped with other regiments of the reserve division under Maj. Gen. McCall, forming the 1ˢᵗ Brigade under the command of Brig. Gen. John F. Reynolds; Division of the Potomac until March of 1862.[1]

Georgetown Heights
Aug. 13, 1861

Dear Father,

Your very welcome letter of the 9ᵗʰ is at hand, and I hasten to answer. On last Saturday our Regiment was taken out on picket.[2] Our company stationed some 4 miles from camp on the plantation of a man who is doubtless[3] a cescessionist [sic] at heart. Seven of his negroes have been away since the war began. The slaves are all strongly for the Union. We remained on picket until Sunday evening. Nothing of importance occurred, and we had but little to do, but just as we were starting home it began raining in torrents. We got wet to the skin and are not dry yet for it is still raining. We are right in the midst of a nest of cescessionists but they are too feeble to do any harm. A night or two since, our guards fired on men who were discovered crawling around in the bushes, but owing to the darkness, the shots did not take effect. Entrenchments are now being thrown up for the defense of the city in case the rebels should succeed in crossing the river. Our whole army is now in motion. On Friday, 10 thousand crossed over into Virginia. To-day the fields may be covered over with soldiers' tents and in the morning not a vestige remain.

All classes are glad that McClellan is in command.[4] Company discipline is much more strict than heretofore and these petty company commanders are not allowed to leave the camp and visit every rum shop in the neighborhood. Oh, but it galls them. All the drinking shops are shut-up near here and the penalty for selling liquor to soldiers is heavy. Every officer is to undergo a strict military examination, woe, woe to captains.

To your questions I answer. 1st, there have been no prayer meetings in camp since we came here. We have been several times absent from camp and are almost constantly moving. 2nd, we have prayers in our tent in the evening. Take turns in leading. 3rd, the 10th Regiment is close to us, but we do not get the chance to visit other Regiments. P. Bessor is here. I have seen him several times. Yesterday I took the men out to fire the loads out of their guns and saw him along the road. 4th, we have received fifteen days' pay. I,

since the late act, receive twenty-two dolls [dollars] per month. 5th,
we have received new guns. Very good muskets. The Harpers Ferry
guns. 6th, some of the men complain a great deal of the captain,
but he treats me very well. He swears a good deal at the men, but
never yet at me. There cannot be a finer man or officer than our
First Lieutenant. The men almost idolize him.

Continue your questions. I shall be most happy to answer
them. There are many things [that] may be interesting to you
which I never think of in writing. I received letters from John[5]
and Lizzie the latter part of last week and answered them both.

We may at any hour have a little brush with the enemy and
have to hold ourselves in readiness to move at a moment['s] warning. My trust is in God and I feel that He will keep me. General
Scott[6] says those who survive shall eat their Christmas[7] dinner at
home. It is very consoling to know that so many prayers are daily
ascending on my behalf.

Your Affectionate Son,

Jamie

Author's Notes

This letter was written on special stationery of the period. It shows a woman wearing a patriotic dress and holding the American flag with the following poem:

> Columbia, Columbia, to glory arise,
> The queen of the world and the child of the skies,
> Thy genius commands thee; with rapture behold,
> While ages on ages thy splendor unfold.

1. sources #1, p. 119; #2, p.756

Maj. Gen. George A. McCall (1802–1868), born in Philadelphia, Pennsylvania, was an 1822 graduate of West Point. At the beginning of the Civil War, he helped to organize the Pennsylvania Volunteers as major general of the state militia and was commissioned brigadier general of the Volunteers in May 1861. He led the Pennsylvania Reserves Division which served in the Army of the Potomac and was one of the oldest West Point graduates to serve in the Civil War. He served in the Peninsula Campaign where he was wounded and captured in June 1862. He was imprisoned and later released in August in a prisoner exchange. Due to poor health, he resigned in March 1863. (source #8)

Brig. Gen. John F. Reynolds (1820–1863) was one of the most highly esteemed Union corps commanders. He was an 1841 West Point graduate and a native of Pennsylvania. At the outbreak of the Civil War, he was an instructor at his alma mater. He was made second in command of the newly organized regular army infantry regiments. He was assigned to the command of a brigade of the Pennsylvania Reserves, which he trained in the Washington area. The division was engaged at Gaines' Mill. The next morning, after being cut off from his troops, Reynolds was captured. In August 1861, he was released on a prisoner exchange in time to command the Pennsylvania Reserves in the defeat at 2nd Bull Run. Reynolds was then put in charge of three corps at Gettysburg and was killed on the first day of fighting. (source #9)

2. A picket was an advance outpost or guard for a large force. Pickets were ordered to form a scattered line far in advance of the main army's encampment, but within supporting distance. A picket guard was made up of a lieutenant, two sergeants, four corporals, and forty privates from each regiment. Picket duty was the most hazardous work of

infantrymen in the field, since these men were the first to encounter any major enemy movement and the most likely target of snipers. Picket duty was rotated, by regulation, in a regiment. (source #11)

3. James's formation of the word "doubtless" is one example of the idiosyncracies of the copperplate or English round-hand style of handwriting. This style evolved in England in the earliest part of the 18th century due to the need for an efficient, commercial hand. Until the middle of the 18th century, the American colonies relied on this handwriting model from England, and it can be seen in the Declaration of Independence. Unique to the copperplate style is the so-called "long S" or "long-tailed S." The lower case "s" (or "ss") character resembled an "f." The roundhand style influenced the American "Spencerian" script taught in schools through-out the United States in the 1840s, and dominated American correspondence until the introduction of the Palmer method of handwriting in the 1920s. There are examples of the "long S" in four of the letters included in the book: "doubtless" in this letter, "bless" on page 51 "less" on page 78, and "blissfull" on page 200. (sources #51 and #52)

4. Two of Maj. Gen. George McClellan's (1826–1885) assign-ments were as commander of the Army and Department of the Potomac (August 15, 1861–November 9, 1862) and

commander-in-chief, U. S. A (November 5, 1861–March 11, 1862). Under his leadership, the Army of the Potomac was transformed into a disciplined fighting force. His men affectionately called him "Little Mac." McClellan quite often overestimated the strength of his enemy. These delays prompted Lincoln to suspend him from command of all the armies in March of 1862, allowing him to concentrate on the movements of the Army of the Potomac and Richmond. Finally, after more demonstrations of delayed action allowed the enemy time to improve their position, the War Department relinquished McClelland's command on November 9, 1862. He returned home awaiting new directives that never came. In 1864 he ran as the Democratic candidate against Lincoln. He served as New Jersey's governor in the late 1870s and early 1880s. (sources #9 and #12)

5. John was James's brother and a Methodist minister.

6. General Winfield Scott (1786–1866), having served his country for two decades, was a preeminent military figure— perhaps the most celebrated since George Washington. When he commanded the Union armies, he was 75 years of age and clearly at the end of his career. He was a Virginia native who refused to join the Confederacy. Scott had asked Lincoln to appoint Robert E. Lee as his field commander. Lee turned it down and the position went to

George McClelland. Scott's "Anaconda Plan," which rec-ommended the use of a naval blockade to put pressure on the Confederacy while the Union troops were developed, was criticized and many felt that Scott was growing senile. He anticipated the war to be a long struggle, unlike the majority of Union and Confederate military and political figures who believed the war would conclude quickly. After another Union defeat at Ball's Bluff, his standing offer to resign was accepted, and he was succeeded that same day by McClellan. Scott lived to see the defeat of the Confederates as well as the success of the essential elements of his Anaconda Plan in waging the war. He was buried at West Point although he never attended there. (source #9)

7. "The war will be over by Christmas." Anonymous. This was a common pronouncement by soldiers in 1861. (source #61, p. 7)

The regiment remained at Tennallytown, Maryland, about two months. The time was passed in camp routine, picket duty, and responding to frequent alarms along the line of the Potomac.[1]

CAMP TENNALLY
SEPTEMBER 7, 1861

Dear Father,

Your very kind letter came safely to hand this evening, and I hasten to answer. I was glad to learn of your safe arrival and that not withstanding you were among many who are opposed to our Country and her hallowed institutions. You had a good and prosperous time. We need no better proof of the righteousness of our cause than the very fact that it is opposed by J. Cummings and others you mentioned. The Devil always did and always will love his own works, but with the God of battles on our side, we fear not all that can be brought against us. I firmly believe that He is overruling for good and to His glory.

The defeat at Manassas,[2] if defeat it may be called, I believe like the storming of Sumter[3] was one of the most providential incidents so far of the war. The North had grown quite lethargic and were fast falling asleep under a mistaken feeling of security, when our Capital, our all, was in greatest danger. But this aroused them and they have poured in like a flood, their brave and gallant fathers, husbands, sons, and brothers, and Washington is, I think, without doubt safe.

On last Wednesday we received orders to put into our haversacks[4] two days' rations and prepare to march. About 9 o'clock our regiment was in motion for the Potomac. The 7th Regiment had been stationed there for 7 or 8 days previous and on the day before we started, they had been schelled[5] out of their quarters by Rebel batteries stationed just across the river. We marched 14 miles and in the evening ours with 2 other companies went on picket on the shores of the river. As we were all expecting the enemy to attempt to cross during the night, none of the men were allowed to sleep, but nothing of importance occurred. In the morning several of the enemy were seen on the opposite bank, and one of them snapped his gun at one of our men, but fortunately it having rained all night his gun did not go off. We had hard work to prevent the men from trying the skill of Penna. marksmen on them, but as the camp would have been alarmed by so doing we durst [dare] not fire.[6]

At night we slept on our blankets in an open field. Lieut. Eichelberger, J. R. Callahan, T. A. Taylor, and myself slept on our 3 gum blankets,[7] while our government blankets we had for a covering. I never slept more sweetly and in the morning when aroused I felt fresh and vigorous.

At about 9 o'clock we started home to Camp Tennally where we arrived about 5 o'clock P.M. and found Jacob Eichelberger and three recruits for our company awaiting our return.

We now number 85 men; we need 16 to fill out our company. I understand a great many hard things have been written home about Captain, most of these are false, childish, and not worthy of countenance. Any one acquainted with Army Regulations must knok[8] that many of these could not be so. Barmond and Whisel are both at Annapolis Junction in Hospital. J. H. Williams is in the Regimental Hospital. He is getting better, but is still very weak. Our sickness I think is on the decrease. My health was never better.

This is Sunday afternoon. I commenced this last night, but had not time to finish it. I was at preaching this morning and listened to a good sermon. We received our overcoats to-day and this afternoon the Regiment went on picket. I have some writing to do and could not go. I am kept quite busy, but am quite comfortable. Our rations are good and all have plenty to eat. For the last few days I have been issuing provisions. I give the men all they want and have more now than I know what to do with.

Dear Father, although I know that danger is around us, yet it seems impossible for any of us to realize our position and we feel as safe here as we would at home. Indeed the most we have to fear is from disease and not from bullets,[9] but my trust I hope is in God. Oh, that we could feel at all times that we are in the hands of a kind and merciful God who will not willingly afflict any of His children.

Our fortifications are now about complete and the cannon are peering with their huge iron heads over the sides.

Give my love to all my friends. I received letters from Jim and Lizzie not long since. They were well. I will write as often as I can.

Your Affectionate Son,

James

We have the nicest and cleanest camp around. [10]

AUTHOR'S NOTES

Company F soldiers: (source #1, p. 122; #2, pp. 764, 774-775; #50; #54; #55)

All of these men mustered into service on 6/19/61. The Company F dates for mustering out vary between May 24 and May 26, 1864. Muster in [or out] means to enlist in or be discharged from military service. (source #6)

Eli Eichelberger, Captain, captured at Gaines' Mill; promoted from 1st Lt., 10/30/63; wounded at Wilderness, 5/6/64; absent in hospital at muster out

Jacob R. Callahan, Sergeant Major, promoted from private to Sergeant, date unknown; re-enlisted 1/25/64, at Alexandria, VA; promoted to Sgt. Maj., 3/1/64; transferred to 191st Regiment P.V., 5/15/64, veteran volunteer

Thomas A. Taylor, Private, mustered out with company 5/24/64

John Barmond, Private, discharged on Surgeon's certificate, 4/24/62

William Whisel, Private, discharged 1/24/63, by reason of wounds and loss of arm at Fredericksburg, Va., Dec. 1862

1. source #1, p. 119; #2, p. 756

2. The Manassas Campaign, also called First Bull Run, took place on July 21, 1861. Total estimated casualties were 4,700 (Union, 2,950 and Confederate, 1,750). This became the first major battle on Virginia soil. The inexperienced Union Army under Brig. Gen. McDowell marched from Washington toward the Confederate Army, located behind Bull Run beyond Centreville. It was here that Thomas Jackson earned his nickname, "Stonewall." The defeated Union Army retreated on the 22nd to Washington. This conflict convinced President Lincoln that the war would be long and costly. McDowell was replaced as the commander of the Union Army by Maj. Gen. McClellan whose duty was to reorganize and train the troops. (source #13)

How battles got their names: The Union usually named battles after the closest stream or river, whereas the Confederates used the nearest town or junction for their battle names. Thus, the South named this battle after Manassas Junction and the North named it for the stream Bull Run. (source #14)

3. Fort Sumter, named after a South Carolina Revolutionary
War hero, is located on a man-made island in the Charleston,
South Carolina, harbor. Maj. Robert Anderson was chosen
by President Buchanan to command the Federal forts in
Charleston Harbor. It is believed that he was appointed
because of his Southern ties. Buchanan was attempting to
avoid actions that might provoke South Carolina. By the
same token, the South thought that Anderson would sympa-
thize with their cause and surrender the forts. Upon taking
command, Anderson requested more reinforcements from
the War Department. Buchanan agreed, but did not send
the reinforcements because of pressure from the Southern
members of his cabinet. Anderson was instructed not to take
any action that would provoke an attack. He believed that by
moving his command from Fort Moultrie to Fort Sumter,
he would avoid bloodshed. This was on December 26, 1860.
After years of growing disagreement between the North and
South, the situation deteriorated on April 12, 1861. Union
soldiers surrendered the fort after 34 hours of resistance.
(sources #15 and #16)

"I here declare my unmitigated hatred to Yankee rule to all
political, social & business connection with Yankees & to the
Yankee race. Would that I could impress these sentiments, in
their full force, on every living southerner, & bequeath them
to every one yet to be born!" —Quoted in *The Civil War and*

Reconstruction: A Documentary Collection, ed. by William E. Gienapp. Edmund Ruffin (1794–1865), who supposedly fired the first shot at Fort Sumter, wrote this in his diary just before committing suicide to avoid living under a U. S. government. (source #61, p. 347)

4. The haversack was a canvas bag about a foot square, which held the Civil War soldier's daily rations. It was slung on a strap over the right shoulder and hung on the left hip. It had a waterproof lining and a flap that buckled over its top. Some officers' and militia models were custom-made of patent leather. They frequently had a number or other company identification painted or stenciled on them." (source #11)

5. British spelling of "shelled" (source #6)

6. In reference to the assistance that the 8th Regiment gave to the 7th , General McCall said, "It numbers 890 men, armed with rifles and muskets of improved patterns. An officer is out recruiting for it [the 8th]. The men are well equipped and well drilled." (source #2, p. 756)

7. Gum blankets: During the 1800s, different materials were being tested to best serve the needs of the military. Goodyear had a patent for the vulcanization of rubber made from gum. This gum rubber was a perfect material for blankets to be

used by the Civil War armies. Rubber blankets and ponchos were used by the military through World War I and beyond. They were perfect as ground cloths or to make "shebangs," the Civil War term for shelter, and could be draped over the body for rain gear. In his Nov. 3, 1861, letter, James gave the gum blanket rave reviews, as it kept him dry while serving guard duty during a torrential downpour. (source #17)

8. knok: colloquial definition of "to deduct" (source #6)

9. While the average soldier thought that the bullet was his most dangerous enemy, disease was the biggest killer in the war. Of the Federal dead, three out of every five died of disease. One of the reasons for the high rate of disease was the slipshod recruiting process that allowed under- or over-age men and those in noticeably poor health to join, especially in the first year. By late 1862, two hundred thousand recruits originally accepted for service were judged physically unfit and were discharged, either because they had fallen ill or their frail condition was discovered in a routine examination. (source #18)

10. At first I thought it was strange that James would comment on the cleanliness of their camp, but he most definitely had a right to brag about such an accomplishment. About half of the deaths during the Civil War were the result of intestinal

disorders such as typhoid fever, diarrhea, and dysentery. Many others died of pneumonia and tuberculosis. Many of the men in camp had not been exposed to a variety of contagious diseases, so there were many outbreaks of measles, chicken pox, mumps, and whooping cough. The culprit of most wartime illness was the filth of many army camps. An inspector in late 1861 found most Federal camps "littered with refuse, food, and other rubbish, sometimes in an offensive state of decomposition." As a result, bacteria and viruses spread rapidly through the camp. Bowel disorders constituted the soldiers' most common complaint. The Union Army reported that more than 995 out of every 1,000 men eventually contracted chronic diarrhea and dysentery during the war. (source #18)

William H. Whisel (circled), with Civil War buddies.
Lost left arm in Battle of Fredericksburg. Became Everett postmaster
in 1869. Great grandfather of Danna L. (Blair) Foor.
Courtesy of Barbara Miller (obtained from Charles Butch Miller)

CAMP TENNALLY
SEPT. 08, 1861

Dear Father,

I wrote you yesterday, but was too late this morning to get it in the mail. To-day some gentlemen from your neighborhood arrived here and as they intend returning in a few days, I think I will send letters by them. My health continues great. Williams and the rest of our men are all improving in health.

Enclosed I send $10.00, also my likeness. Nothing of importance has occurred lately. Our Regiment is in General Reynolds's brigade. With much love to all, I am

Your Affectionate Son,

Jamie

I will write to Mother as soon as I find time. I will send her a paper tomorrow.

thing is torn up and left in a perfect Chaos even private letters are scattered around in every direction. Some of which, right or wrong, I read, wishing to learn something of the history of the former residents. The old man was a preacher and physician, his son was a lawyer. The letters I read were all written in a very fine style. Were mostly from the son to his parents and sisters and were full of tenderness, piety and affection.

Oh the sad devastation that was thus made. I could sit and weep over the ruin of this once happy but deserted home. The crops are all left without a husbandman to gather them, and the flocks without a shepherd. Oh! unhappy, misled, and infatuated Virginia. Why did she leave the fostering, sheltering fold of the Union? And unite with reckless and ambitious men, who will not spare even their neighbor's fireside, for the ... army spares not the substance of either friend or foe

The second page of James's October 11, 1861, letter

On the 9ᵗʰ of October, the regiment moved across the stream and took position with the Camp Army of the Potomac at Camp Pierpont (Langley, VA). This became their winter quarters until March 10, 1862.[1]

PROSPECT HILL
OCTOBER 11, 1861

Dear Father,

You see by this that we are no longer at Camp Tennally. We left there on Wednesday evening at dark, crossed the chain bridge, and are now about 6 miles in Virginia, further than any of our troops have heretofore been in this direction. To-day our company with five others of our Regiment are on advance picket. The cavalry pickets are about 100 yards in advance.

We have taken up headquarters in a house formerly occupied by a cescesssionist, but now left in sole possession of an old negro, his wife, and two grandchildren. All of the furniture was left in the house, consisting of household furniture very rich but ancient. All left even to the carpet and crockery, an excellent library consisting of a large selection of choice books such as <u>Butler's Analogy</u>,[2] the Wesleyan Offering, Watson, Text and Altar, medical works, etc. But everything is torn up and left in a perfect chaos; even private letters are scattered around in every direction—some of which, right or wrong, I read, wishing to learn something of the history of the former residents. The old man was a preacher and a physician. His son was a lawyer. The letters I read were all written in a very fine style, were mostly from the son to his parents and sisters, and were full of tenderness, piety, and affection.

Oh, the sad devastation that war has made. I could sit and weep over the ruin of this once happy, but deserted home. The crops are all left without a husbandman to gather them, and the flocks without a shepherd. Oh, unhappy, misled and infatuated Virginia. Why did she leave the fostering sheltering fold of the Union? And unite with reckless and ambitious men who will not spare even their neighbor's fireside, for the cescesssion army spared not the substance of either friend or foe.

Even the old clock is thrown in among a heap of rubbish here, and I suppose a bushel of letters, which should have been private and sacred, are left loose around the house and exposed to the perusal of all. The old arm chair covered and cushioned stands in the bed room in which I am now writing, and one thinks could its occupant, probably an aged grandmother, look down from her peaceful home in heaven she would shed tears, if the angels weep, at the ruin around. It is consoling to me to know that while I am here, my dear parents, brother, and sister are safe at home.

The day before we came here there were some 6 or 7 thousand cecession troops at this place, but fled before the approach of our army. It is more than probable that we will not return to our old camp, but push onward into Virginia. May God go with us and give to our arms success.

It is now more than four months since I left home, but my time has been so entirely with my duties that it seems but yesterday we parted. Time hangs heavily only on the hands of the idle. Do not think that I forget home, for my thoughts are constantly there and I care not who it is, if he has the heart of a man and is away from home and loved ones under such circumstances as we are, he will often pause and wander far away in thought and in imagination, live over again his home and fireside scenes, but yet a sense of duty urges me on the steps I have. I pray <u>God</u> that I may be a centenarian by no other motive.

We still have good food and frequently get little extras in the shape of vegetables dug from the deserted gardens around the camp. One of the men has just brought me a nice dish of potatoes already roasted. They were very nice.

My address will still be the same as heretofore. I will write as often as I can. Sometimes I may be so situated that I cannot write for a week or two. Write me often as convenient. Remember me kindly to Jim.

Your Affectionate Son,

James

Author's Notes

1. source #1, p. 119; source #2, p. 756

2. This is probably a reference to Joseph Butler's infamous *Analogy of Religion, Natural and Revealed, to the Constitution and Course of Nature*, written in 1736. In his book, Butler states his view that under normal circumstances humans are designed to live moral lives. His work impressed John Wesley, founder of Methodism, and was read widely in Scotland at the end of the 18th century. It made its way to Oxford and American institutions in the early 19th century. It became part of the curriculum of Dickinson College when it reopened under the presidency of John Durbin. This undertaking was in keeping with the drive of the Methodist Church to support and purify American higher education. Durbin's leadership set out to change the academic program that would require students to engage in courses in religion and ethics. Studying Butler's *Analogy* became a requirement of all second-semester seniors. After Durbin's tenure as president, Butler's *Analogy* became the subject of much controversy. However, it remained a part of the curriculum for 45 years, appearing in the 1895–96 Dickinson catalogue for the last time. (source #19)

Camp Pierpont
October 22, 1861

Dear Father,

I should have answered John's letter at home immediately, but it was not received until late on Friday evening, and before daylight Saturday morning we were called out and marched some 12 or 15 miles farther into Virginia towards Leesburg. We went with quite a large force consisting of 4 Regiments of infantry, one of cavalry, and 2 or three batteries of artillery. As soon as we got outside of our pickets, our company was thrown out as scouts and skirmishers. The country was very rough, and we had to extend about one mile on each side of the road. Traveling through the woods, over hills, and through swamps and briars most of the time running was not by any means easy work. I had charge of the second platoon of the company and the left side of the road. My men stood it well, but Linn had to throw his shirt away. We halted just before dusk in the evening and our company was ordered again out on picket. By this time the Capt. was played out, as the boys call it, and I had to take charge of the company. The men came up to the work nobly, indeed beyond expectation, and we started out with a right good will, but after marching a mile or so across the fields, we were hastily called in and learned that the whole brigade had marched a mile and a half further than ordered, and we had to march back. Finally we halted about 9 o'clock, encamped in the woods, and soon were sound asleep. I was scarcely asleep before the lieut. came and wakened me up with the orders to put on a guard, relieving him every two hours through the night, and at day break start the fires, arouse the Reg., and then awaken him so that we could get breakfast and be ready to be under arms at sunrise. We had driven the enemy's pickets on before us so that we had to watch close for fear of surprise. My corporal assisted me through the night so that I got 4 or 5 hours sleep.

In the morning our company was again ordered on advance picket duty. (This seemed hard, but under circumstances was fair.) I placed my furthest picket post at a house occupied by a family named Jenkins. There was no one there but the lady of the house, two daughters about the ages of 19 and 12 years and a son about 15. The gentleman and an older son had left and the lady of the house left during the afternoon. The daughter I found to be quite intelligent, sociable, and witty and handsome, and I spent most of my time at the house and very agreeably too, talking politics, condition of the country, etc, etc. In the evening T. A. Taylor and myself partook of an excellent supper prepared by her. The rest of the boys, although invited, did not eat any.

She professed to be a secessionist, but before I left I suspected she was doing it more for the fun of the thing than otherwise. She stated that there had been a great many Union men in the neighborhood, but had to flee the rebel army and take refuge north. Indeed we saw but one or two men in our march. The Louisiana Rebel Regiments have behaved most shamefully in the vicinity, destroying property, breaking by force into houses, ravishing women, etc. At first several families fled at our approach expecting the same treatment, but soon returned when they found that we came not to destroy but to protect and many were glad to see us.

On Monday we returned to camp Pierpont very tired but well pleased with our trip. After the Regiment was dismissed the Colonel called our Capt., Lieut., and myself to his quarters to thank us personally for the manner in which our company performed its very and extraordinarily severe duties. He said nothing that has transpired since he has entered the service has given him so much pleasure. I hope we may ever do our duty. May God assist us, and may we give to Him the Glory.

We have now 7 men in hospital, but they are doing finely. Oh how thankful I ought to be to God for the perseverance of my health for we have vastly more to fear from disease than from the enemy....

Although there is no subsequent page or closing to this letter, the following is a single page marked "continued" that may perhaps complete the above letter. It too has no closing. Based on James's last sentence, I believe that this "continued" second page could have been written at the time of the Battle of Ball's Bluff near Leesburg on October 21, 1861. The paper is engraved with a six-pointed star. The points of the star are striped red, white, and blue. There are smaller stars between the points and a picture of McClellan in the center. Under the star it reads, "Commander of the Federal forces on the Potomac."

J. H. Williams has joined us at camp. Looks well, but is not yet fit for duty. I think he will write to the Run to-day. It is quite likely we will be moving a good deal now. I may not be able to write very often, but I will write as often as I have opportunity and may God bless us all, keep and preserve us by his Almighty power. We are all in His hands and not one can fall without His notice. Give my love to Mother and to all my friends at the Run.

There are now 12 thousand rebel troops in Leesburg, but before long I think it will be in our hands.

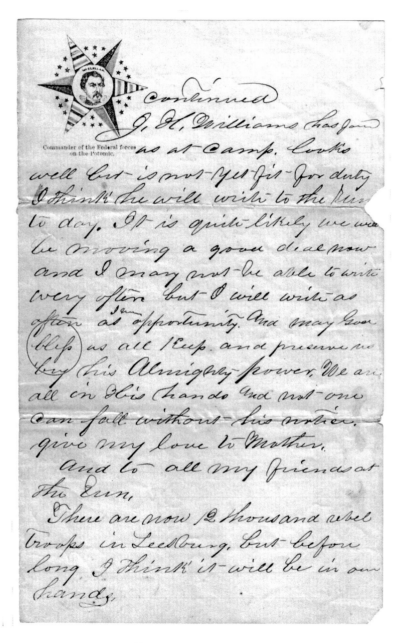

Commander of the Federal forces
on the Potomic;

Continued

J, H, Williams has Joined
us at Camp. looks
well but is not yet fit for duty
I think he will write to the Run
to day. It is quite likely we will
be moving a good deal now
and I may not be able to write
very often but I will write as
often as opportunity. And may God
bless us all Keep. and preserve us
by his Almighty power, We are
all in His hands And not one
can fall without his notice.
give my love to Mother.

And to all my friends at
the Run,

There are now 12. thousand rebel
troops in Leesburg, but before
long I think it will be in our
hands,

James's "continued" letter
Note the "long S" in "bless" (circled)

Author's Notes

Company F soldier: (source #1, p. 122; #2, p. 774; #54; #55)

Jacob B. Linn, Sergeant, mustered into service 6/19/61; promoted from Private to Corporal; promoted to Sergeant, 3/1/64; mustered out with company 5/24/64

CAMP PIERPONT
NOVEMBER 3, 1861

Dear Father,

I received yours on Friday evening and should have answered it immediately, but had to start on Grand Guard[1] or picket duty before daylight Saturday morning. I arose at three o'clock, called up the men, took breakfast, and started. It had rained all night and still it continued to rain in torrents and did not cease until morning so that we had a muddy tramp and a very disagreeable time being out 30 hours without shelter, but thanks to my gum blanket I did not get very wet. I do not know how I could do without it. It is perfectly waterproof and by using it as a cape and wearing my gum skull cap, I can keep my body dry. Let it rain never so hard. I think it has already preserved me from many colds and perhaps fever. To-day I feel very sleepy as well as fatigued. With this exception I am well. I often think that I ought to be very thankful to God that He has preserved my health so that while so many have been sick and numbers died of disease I have ever been able to attend to my duties.

I am sorry to learn of the pains in your hip and knee. <u>I do hope</u> it may result in nothing serious, but until I hear from you again I am uneasy. If you are unable to write, please get someone to write and let me know how you are. Our Regiment will, I think, be paid now in the course of a week or ten days. When we receive it, I will immediately send some home.

We cannot conjecture what will be done with us this winter or where our quarters will be, but we are willing to trust the wisdom and skill of McClellan. General Scott has resigned. The hero, kind, great General and wise counsellor has almost run his race. May he in his last days be true to his God as he has ever been to his country. May his last moments be peaceful and happy. Before he closes his life [may he] see the restoration of peace and prosperity to our country and receive at last a crown of glory surpassing all that mortals can bestow.

In McClellan we hope he has a worthy successor and Heaven grant that he may prove such. The report circulated [illegible] relative to our Captain is basely false. He never has been court-martialed and is not likely to be.

I wrote you a letter acknowledging the receipt of the quilt from Mother and the stockings from Esq. Peebles. As you did not get it, it must have been miscarried. Please return my warmest thanks for them, for they were just the things I needed and add much to my comfort.

The letter you mention from Ben Peebles I did not receive. I received a letter from Rev. Chenowith requesting me to search for a Ben Chenowith in the 16th Indiana Regiment, but I am not near it and consequently could not possibly find him or I would do so. Last Sunday I heard Ben Consor preach.[2] He is in the 5th Regiment and in our Brigade stationed close to us. Return my regards to Dr. Mann and wife. With love to all friends, I am

Your Affectionate Son,

Jamie

I must now get an hour's sleep.

AUTHOR'S NOTES

1. Grand Guard (mil.): one of the posts of the second line belonging to a system of advance posts of an army. (source #39)

2. Chaplain S. L. M. Consor, Field and Staff Officer of the 34th PA Regiment, 5th Reserve; mustered out by Special Order of War Department on 11/1/62 (source #2, p. 673; #55)

CAMP PIERPONT, VIRGINIA
NOVEMBER 10, 1861

Dear Father,

On Tuesday or Wednesday I will send you by express $25.00. Please write me immediately on its reception so that I may be sure you get it. All is quiet here and we are getting along fine.

I would send you more money, but I want to purchase boots, for we get only shoes for the winter, also a pair of gloves, etc. This I think necessary for the preservation of my health, of which I am very careful.

Pray for me.

The news of the day is all cheering. With much love to all, I am

Your Affectionate Son,

Jamie

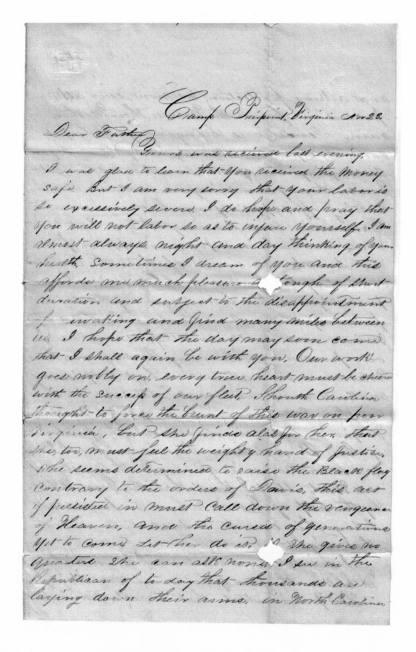

Camp Pierpont, Virginia Nov 23.

Dear Father,

Yours was received last evening.
I was glad to learn that you received the money
safe. But I am very sorry that your labor is
so excessively severe. I do hope and pray that
you will not labor so as to injure yourself. I am
almost always. night and day thinking of your
health. Sometimes I dream of you and this
affords me much pleasure a though of short
duration and subject to the disappointment
of waking and find many miles between
us. I hope that the day may soon come
that I shall again be with you. Our work
goes nobly on. every true heart must be cheered
with the success of our fleet. South Carolina
thought to force the brunt of this war on poor
Virginia, but she finds alas for her, that
she, too, must feel the weighty hand of Justice,
she seems determined to raise the Black flag
contrary to the orders of Davis, this act
of persisted in must call down the vengeance
of Heaven, and the curses of generations
yet to come Let her do it. if she gives no
quarter she can ask none. I see in the
Republican of to-day that thousands are
laying down their arms, in North Carolina

James's November 23, 1861, letter

CAMP PIERPONT, VIRGINIA
NOV. 23, 1861

Dear Father,

Yours was received last evening. I was glad to learn that you received the money safe, but I am very sorry that your labor is so excessively severe. I do hope and pray that you will not labor so as to injure yourself. I am almost always night and day thinking of your health. Sometimes I dream of you and this affords me much pleasure although of short duration and subject to the disappointment of waking and find[ing] many miles between us. I hope that the day may soon come that I shall again be with you.

Our work goes nobly on. Every true heart must be cheering with the success of our fleet. South Carolina thought to force the brunt of this war on poor Virginia, but she finds, alas for her, that she too must feel the weighty hand of justice. She seems determined to raise the black flag[1] contrary to the orders of Davis.[2] This act, if persisted in, must call down the vengeance of Heaven and the curses of generations yet to come. Let her do it. If she gives no quarters she can ask none.

I see in the *Republican*[3] of to-day that thousands are laying down their arms in North Carolina and asking protection and none ever asked protection from the Union, their Mother, in vain. Tennessee is bringing forth loyal sons daily. Already they have begun destroying the great South Western railroad, thereby rendering us material aid in cutting off supplies from Richmond and Manassas and leaving them but two roads over which to procure supplies from the south. One of these coast roads connecting Richmond with Charleston has probably ere this been seized by the land forces of the expedition. The third and minor one will doubtless soon be in our possession, leaving Richmond and Manassas no alternative but to yield or make a mad and rash attack on us here on the Potomac. The people of Accomac, Virginia, have in obedience to the proclamation from Gen. Dix,[4] declared themselves for the Union and so our cause is gaining, North, South, East, and West. I think that the great McClellan by the help of <u>God</u> in whom he trusts will bring this war to a successful issue[5] and that right speedily.

I think Abraham Lincoln[6] and Gen. B. McClellan the two great men now living. How providential that we elected Lincoln when we did. Had we elected any one of the other candidates, as their recent course plainly proves, we would now be a broken and divided nation, the scorn and contempt of the whole world, and [would have] demonstrated to all nations that a Republican Government and institutions cannot stand.

Last Wednesday we had the greatest review of troops that ever took place in the United States.[7] The review took place at Baileys cross roads. 70,000 soldiers were presented. When I look over this living, moving mass of true and loyal men all sworn and willing if needs be to sacrifice their lives, their all, in defense of the Constitution and the Union, my heart swelled within me. I felt proud that I was one of the units of which the whole was composed. Here it was in the ranks that could be seen true patriotism. An officer may be influenced to deeds of daring by selfish ambition, but the private falls and is unnoticed and unsung. They suffer many privations the officer never experiences, and yet they do it cheerfully for their country, rewarded by the knowledge that they are on the side of justice and of right.

At the review, there were thousands of spectators from Washington, and the scene was most grand and imposing, but of this you can learn more from the papers than I can write. On the way to the review ground we passed Lewynsville[sic], Falls Church, Ball's Cross Roads,[8] and Munson Hill,[9] places all known as the scenes of skirmishes between the forces and the rebels.

This morning our company came in from Grand Guard duty. I was not out. I felt rather unwell and staid[sic] in to rest. Now I again feel well and am fit for duty. Neither Captain or Lieutenant have resigned. The Lieutenant is well and Captain's getting better. Isaiah M. Davis from Pattonsville is dangerously sick and from present appearance will not recover.

You misunderstood my last [letter] in regards to your solicitude for me. I did not think you were wrong in your kind counsel, but only meant to say that I would not be rash or careless. But there is no danger here. We are not very near the enemy.

Give my love to Mother and remember me to all the friends, Bro. Moore,[10] Barndollars, Williams, Peebles, Dr. Mann, Masters, and all others.

Your Very Affectionate Son,

James

Author's Notes

Company F soldier: (source #1, p. 122; #2, p. 774; #54; #55)

Isaiah M. Davis, Private, mustered into service 6/19/61; died at Camp Piermont, Virginia, 11/28/61

1. To raise the black flag was a well-known symbol of a ruthless combat, characterized by giving no quarter (mercy) to the enemy. (source #20)

2. Jefferson Davis (1808–1889) was president of the Confederate States of America and commander-in-chief of its army and navy. At the defeat and surrender of the armies of Lee and Johnson, President Davis was made a captive by the military, imprisoned in chains, and charged unjustly with various crimes. After two years' imprisonment, he was released on bond. He was never brought to trial, which he had earnestly demanded. Throughout the rest of his life he remained an opposer of power centralized in the federal government. (source #9)

"The war of the Revolution was successfully waged, and resulted in the treaty of peace with Great Britain in 1783, by the terms of which the several states were *each by name* recognized to be independent." (Speech to a special session of Confederate Congress, April 29, 1861.) Davis was using history to support the right of individual states to leave the Union. (source #61, p. 62)

3. *The Republican*: This is most likely a reference to the local paper, *The Everett Republican*.

4.   General Dix (1798-1879) served as a New York senator and governor of New York. President James Buchanan appointed him U. S. Secretary of the Treasury in 1861. At the start of the war, Dix sent a telegram to the Treasury agents in New Orleans ordering, *"If any one attempts to haul down the American flag, shoot him on the spot."* The telegram was intercepted by Confederates and never delivered, but the text was printed in the press. Dix became one of the first heroes of the North during the Civil War. When the war broke out, he was appointed a major general in the New York Militia. He joined the Union Army as the highest ranking major general of the volunteers during the war, effective May 16, 1861. That winter, he commanded a regional organization known as "Dix's Command" within Maj. Gen. McClellan's Department of the Potomac. Considered too old for field

command, he is credited with the suppression of the New York Draft Riots in July 1863. James mentions the riots in his July 18, 1863, letter. (source #21)

5. issue, meaning "result" (source #6)

6. Abraham Lincoln (1809-1865) In November 1860, against three other names on the ballot (Douglas, Breckinridge, and Bell), Lincoln won the presidential election with only 40% of the popular vote. When inaugurated in March 1861, the Confederate State of America had been formed. With little formal education, this frontier lawyer held the nation together during the worst crisis in its history. In his second inaugural, he shared his views for the restoration of the American union with words like "malice toward none" and "charity for all." Unfortunately his dream was ended just a few weeks later by an assassin's bullet. (source #9, #66)

7. The following information comes from the December 7, 1861, issue, page 779, of *Harper's Weekly*, considered the most popular newspaper during the Civil War: More than twenty generals, commanding divisions and brigades, with five times the number of staff officers, mounted upon high mottled and richly caparisoned horses. After the arrival of the President and Cabinet and Commander-in-Chief, preparation was made for marching the troops in review. The honor of leading

the column was assigned to the First Rifle Regiment of Pennsylvania Reserve, familiarly known as the "Bucktail Regiment." Under the management of General McDowell, some three hours were occupied by the troops in passing with no less than seventy thousand men, including seven regiments of cavalry, numbering some eighty thousand men, and twenty batteries of artillery, numbering a hundred and twenty pieces.

8. Ball's Cross Roads has been a focal point since about 1740, when two roads were developed leading to Alexandria and Falls Church, Virginia.: North Glebe Road and Wilson Boulevard respectively. The intersection became known as Ball's Cross Roads when Ball's Tavern was established there in the early 1800s and is the oldest crossroads in Northern Virginia. (source #23)

9. Munson or Munson's Hill is about five miles from the Chain Bridge, on the northern side of the Leesburg Turnpike, about one mile from Bailey's Crossroads and about three miles from Falls Church. (source # 22)

10. Bro. Moore is a reference to Rev. J. G. Moore who served at the Everett Methodist Church with James's father.

CAMP PIERPONT, VIRGINIA
NOVEMBER ___, 1861

Dear Father,

Yours came to hand night before last. I hope your pains may soon vanish. I am glad your labors are successful and hope that the members will yet pay you up. I know these are hard times, but I always believe that true patriotism begins in the church of God, and I very much doubt the patriotism of the man who will let the church suffer. They may talk, boast, and give, but self, that god of so many, is at the bottom of all. You requested a list of all sick in our company. I here give it.

Wm D. Ritchey at Baltimore, <u>nearly well</u>

Bartlay Manspeaker at Washington, <u>walking about</u>

Frank Dean at Baltimore, (now well) <u>acting as nurse</u>

Zopher Horton at Baltimore, (well) <u>acting as nurse</u>

Aaron Imes, <u>went to hospital yesterday</u>

Sergeant Armstrong, with company, <u>rheumatism, walking about</u>

T.A. Taylor, <u>with company, getting well</u>

David Manspeaker, <u>with company, nearly well</u>

Aaron Foster, <u>walking about, not bad</u>

Sergeant Williams and Callahan, both well and returned to duty

Joseph Ritchey has the rheumatism and will be discharged. I have his discharge filled out and they are now waiting to be signed.

You seem to think we have hard times sleeping on the ground. We never mind that and sleep as sweetly as we would in a bed of down. As for staying up at night, I never mind that and never seem to realize any inconveniences from it. Some of the men put on long faces and whine, but I have never yet been so situated that I could not take a hearty laugh. Some of the men tell me that they don't believe anything could hurt me. This kind of life agrees with me much better than teaching school. I am getting fat and am comfortable. The only thing we need is social intercourse.[1] The news from the fleet as well as from the West is very cheering.

I do not believe, as a good many suppose, we will ever attack Manassas. It is doubtless so well fortified that we could not take it without the loss of 25 or 30 thousand men, and I cannot see what good it would do us if we had it.

Last night all the companies of our Regiment except G and F were taken out to guard a bridge 6 miles from here and were out all night. For once our company was left in camp. Most of the men seem very anxious for battle, but I suppose our generals will know when the proper time comes to strike and Heaven grant it may be successful.

I am glad that the ladies of the Run are doing all they can for the cause. May Heaven bless them and return their husbands, brothers, sons, and friends to them in safety.

Father, you seem constantly to fear I shall act rashly and in so doing fall into the enemy's hands. I shall ever endeavor to act with cool discretion, but I do hope never to prove cowardly. I know you would rather lose me than have me return a disgraced coward. But I shall trust God, without whose notice not even a sparrow can fall,[2] for sustaining power and hope yet to return home and without disgracing our name.

I forgot to say Capt. Eichelberger is still sick, but fast getting better. Give my love to Mother and all our friends. Place no confidence in reports that are circulated through the county. I learn that rumor in Bedford County has had several of our men dead who have never really been sick. I sent twenty-five dolls by Adam's Express yesterday. Please write me as soon as you receive it. I got a letter from Joe McMurray, as Stewart and Miss Mollie Kirby were to be married next week. <u>Strange but true</u>.

Your Very Affectionate Son,

Jamie

Maryland is safe for the Union, not much credit to her.[3]

Author's Notes

Company F soldiers: (source #1, p. 122; #2, pp. 774-775 and Vol. V, pp. 322-323; #54; #55)

All of these men mustered into service on 6/19/61.

D. B. Armstrong, 1st Sergeant, promoted from Sergeant; captured at Gaines' Mill; mustered out with company 5/26/64

B. Manspeaker, Private, killed in action at Fredericksburg, VA, 12/13/62

David Manspeaker, Private, killed in action at Spotsylvania Court House, 5/13/64

Aaron Foster, Private, captured at Gaines' Mill; wounded at Wilderness 5/8/64; mustered out with company 5/26/64

Franklin Dean, Private, wounded at Antietam; discharged, 2/7/63

Aaron Imes, Private, wounded at Fredericksburg; discharged on Surgeon's Certificate, 12/16/63

Joseph Ritchey, Private, discharged on Surgeon's Certificate, 2/26/62

Wm. D. Ritchey, Corporal, prisoner from May 8–12, 1864; transferred to 191st Regiment P. V., Company H, 5/15/64; mustered out with company 6/28/65, veteran volunteer

Zopher P. Horton, Private, transferred to 191st Regiment P. V., Company H 5/15/64; promoted to Corporal 6/13/65; mustered out with company 6/28/65, veteran volunteer

P. V. stands for Pennsylvania Volunteers

1. intercourse, meaning "communication" or "dealings between people" (source #6)

2. Luke 12:7 "Indeed, the very hairs on your head are all numbered. Don't be afraid; you are worth more than many sparrows." (*New International Version*)

3. Maryland did not secede from the Union; however when Union soldiers marched through the city at the start of the war, Confederate sympathizers attacked the troops, which led to the Baltimore riot of 1861. Four soldiers and twelve civilians were killed, which caused Union troops to occupy Baltimore. Maryland came under federal administration—in part, to prevent the state from seceding—until the end of the war. (source #62)

Camp Pierpont Dec 8
1861

Dear Father

For several days I
have not been well, I am
not however seriously ill,
I will take care of myself, And
I think in a day or two I shall
be fully recovered. I am a great
deal better now than I have been,
To day I was over at the Fifth
Regiment to hear Cross or preach
I staid for dinner with him
he inquired kindly concerning
us, I had a long talk with
him. and spent the time very
pleasantly, Our Capt, is again
quite poorly, We have now but
3 men in the hospital and they
are doing well, We are encamped
on disagreable, unwholesome
ground And I hope we may

James's December 8, 1861, letter

CAMP PIERPONT
DECEMBER 8, 1861

Dear Father,

For several days I have not been well. I am not however seriously ill. I will take care of myself, and I think in a day or two I shall be fully recovered. I am a great deal better now than I have been.

To-day I was over at the Fifth Regiment to hear Consor preach. I staid for dinner with him and he inquired kindly concerning you. I had a long talk with him and spent the time very pleasantly. Our Captain is again quite poorly. We have now but 5 men in the hospital and they are doing well. We are camped on disagreeable, unwholesome ground, and I hope we may soon leave. I would far rather meet the enemy on the battle field than disease here.

I do hope Congress will act with wisdom, discrimination, and justice. It seems now as though nothing but the total overthrow of slavery and southern Aristocracy can bring this war to a successful terminus and although at first I was utterly opposed to a war directly against slavery, I now go in for it with heart and hand even though every man, woman, and child of the vile southern Aristocracy should have to be slain. Democracy and Aristocracy cannot live together in the United States. <u>Let Democracy live and the people rule.</u>

I like Jim Lane's and Colonel Cochrane's[1] speeches, and I long now to see every negro south of the Mason Dixon line free and emancipated and this will undoubtedly be the end of the struggle. <u>May God in Mercy hasten the day</u>.

This is the course things by the guidance of <u>Infinite Wisdom</u> have taken, and I firmly believe any man who advocates anything different is a traitor at heart both to <u>God and</u> his country and would rather see the Nation's shame and overthrow than the downfall of that accursed enemy of free and popular institutions (Slavery).

We have been kept here now a good while and the men are all most anxious to leave and move onward. I hope and pray the order may soon come. I am tired of the sickening sympathy with the feelings of traitors and would most gladly crush them and blot them out forever. From the foregoing do not deem me malicious and revengeful. I scorn such motives, but I do want to see Our Country's honor vindicated and her Institutions protected. With much love to all, I am

Your Affectionate Son,

Jamie

There is a company from Clearfield in the fifth Regiment. Larrimer is Captain and John Bigler Lieutenant.

Author's Notes

34th PA Regiment, 5th Reserve, Company C (source #2, pp. 672, 677, 680; #55)

J. Harvey Larrimer, Major, mustered in 5/15/61; promoted from 1st Lt. of Company C to Captain of Company E, 7/12/61; to Major, 5/1/63; killed at Bristoe Station, 2/14/64

John W. Bigler, 2nd Lt., mustered in 6/21/61; resigned on 6/22/62

1. James Henry Lane was actively involved in the abolitionist movement in Kansas in 1855. He is thought by some to have been the leader of the Jayhawkers, a Free Soil militant group, which was successful in getting Kansas admitted to the Union in 1861 as a free state. Lane was elected one of the state's first U. S. senators. (source #43)

    Col. John Cochrane was a member of the Sixty-Fifth Regiment New York, which was organized in July 1861 and better known as the "First United States Chasseurs." They first reached Washington in August 1861, and were immediately sent across the Chain Bridge, where they became involved in the action at Dranesville. Col. John Cochrane (who later became an attorney-general of New York State) was in command. This regiment participated with McClellan in the Peninsula Campaign. (source #24) been killed by the careless handling of loaded guns and it is a great wonder there have not been many more it is almost impossible even by constant watching to get the men to be careful.

The comrade of this man mourns the act most bitterly for they were old associates at home, but his mourning comes too late. unless it be a warning to others. The weather here now is most healthy and pleasant, the nights are quite frosty. And it is very invigorating to breathe the fresh morning air, while the days are quite warm. We have had a general cleaning up around the camp, and I hope there will be less sickness in future. There is not a dangerous patient in the hospital at this time. Capt Eichelberger

The second page of James's December 15, 1861, letter
Note the "long S" in "less" (circled)

CAMP PIERPONT
DEC. 15, 1861

Dear Father,

To-day my heart is full. Inspection over at 9 A.M. When I had made out my morning report of the company, I went over to the fifth Regiment where at 11 A.M. I took the sacrament and renewed my covenant vows with Almighty God. I do hope by my walk and conversation to be instrumental of good. My health has returned, and I am now well as ever. We have beside the Captain but two men sick, and they are getting better. Oh, may the lives of our men be preserved. On Thursday a man belonging to the Regiment was shot through the head by the carelessness of his comrade, making the third who has been killed by the careless handling of loaded guns. It is a great wonder there have not been many more. It is almost impossible even by constant watching to get the men to be careful. The comrades of this man mourn the act most bitterly for they were old associates at home, but his mourning comes too late unless it be a warning to others.

The weather here now is most healthy and pleasant. The nights are quite frosty, and it is very invigorating to breathe the fresh morning air while the days are quite warm. We have had a general cleaning up around the camp, and I hope there will be less sickness in future. There is not a dangerous patient in the hospital at this time. Capt. Eichelberger, I think, will soon leave for home on furlough, remaining some 15 or 20 days to recruit his health, which has not been good since we came across the river. Our Chaplain has not come back yet, and it is probable we will remain here this winter. So long as I remain well, I do not mind this, but when I was unwell I wanted to be moving.

I hope you may soon be well of the pains in your hip and knee and that it may result in nothing serious.

It is a sweet consolation to me at all times to think of home and feel assured that my nearest and dearest ties are all in the army of Emanuel and constantly offering up prayers in my behalf. This assurance buoys up my heart, and in the hour of temptation forms a strong bulwark and tower of defense. I trust in God to bring me of more than conqueror[1] "through Him that has loved me and given himself for me," and I hope yet again to see you all in the flesh to gladden each other's hearts and be your support and stay in declining life. No one can tell how I long for this. This hope has filled my heart for years. May God grant it to be so. I believe I have no sordid selfish object in life and as far as individually concerned would ask not to stay!

But I am sure God knows what is best and rules with a merciful hand. May all be done to His glory. With much love to all, I am

Your Very Affectionate Son,

Jamie

Author's Note

1. James's letters made frequent references to scripture. Although the meaning of this sentence is not quite clear here, he may be alluding to Romans 8:37, which says: "No, in all these things we are more than conquerors through him who loved us." *(New International Version)*

This letter was written one day after the Battle of Dranesville. The 8th Reserve was not a part of it because they were on a reconnaissance to Difficult Creek.[1]

CAMP PIERPONT, VA
SATURDAY EVENING, DEC 21, 1861

Dear Father,

Your very kind letter is at hand this evening [and] finds me quite well and in excellent spirits. I am very happy to learn of the great work the Lord is doing in your midst and very glad that Samuel Williams has found salvation. Tell him to prove faithful and prove himself a valiant soldier for Christ.

Yesterday morning we went with the division on a foraging expedition toward Dranesville.[2] Our Brigade however was marched off the main road about 2 miles up Difficult Creek when we formed line, stacked our guns, and laying by them until about 1 o'clock pm when we heard heavy cannonry in the direction of Dranesville. Were immediately called to arms, and in less time than it takes to write it we were on our way double quick to the scene of action, but much to our regret got there just as the fight was ended and the rebels routed. The particulars of the fight you have [read] before this through the public prints.

It was rather a hard day's work for us although we did not fight. As soon as we learned that there was fighting going on and we might be needed, a shout went up from the lines that made the air ring again and off we struck. No one seemed tired or willing to be left behind. When we came to the creek, we waited not to cross around by the bridge but plunged through the water over our knees and on up the hill as fast as we could run, and I think we traveled 8 or 10 miles about as quick as troops often do.

On the way we passed several wounded soldiers returning to camp. One poor fellow was lying in the fence corner shot through the leg. Two shot through the right arm. One had two bullets through one arm and although the surgeon told him it would be necessary to amputate it, he was merry and jovial as though it were the most trifling thing in the world. Another shot through the breast was walking to camp without assistance, stopped and showed us the place where the bullet entered, which was about two inches inside the right nipple and nearly the center of the breast and was taken out of his back by the surgeon. "But ah," said he, "we paid them well for all this." They in fact were all in the best of spirits and seemed to regard it as a glorious thing to bleed for their Country. Even some poor fellows who could just raise their heads from the litters would look up and smile with apparent pleasure. We also passed 3 prisoners that were being brought in. They were dirty hard-looking cases and as they passed by us looked very much as I should suppose a dog would that had been caught stealing sheep. We halted close to the battle ground and staid until all our wounded and dead were brought in.[3] And the Regiment that had been in the fight passed us.

Nearly everyone had a secession buiscuit [sic] on his bayonet and most of them loaded with booty such as guns, boots, shoes, blankets, overcoats, canteens, haversacks, etc. They were all elated with their victory, but spoke of fighting as something not very desirable and one almost wept as he related how his comrade was shot dead by his side. It was doubtless a hand fight. The Bucktails[4] are said to have fought most desperately. Col. Kane was badly wounded but still rode at the head of his men, urging them on until the bugle called him from the chase. The Rebels left Leesburg very early in the morning doubtless expecting an easy victory, but they ran against a snag and many of them who were buoyant and hopeful in the morning bit the dust before night.

At dark we started to camp where we arrived about 11 o'clock quite tired, having marched about 25 miles. Thus much I have seen of war, but have not yet been in a fight.

I send you enclosed some crumbs of secession bread. There is no salt in it, but a great deal of saleratus.[5] Taste it. It is after my bedtime. Good night.

Your Affectionate Son,

Jamie

AUTHOR'S NOTES

1. source #1, p. 119; #2, p. 757

2. With winter approaching, sufficient food and rations for the men and forage for the thousands of horses and mules was an ever-present concern. Five days before Christmas, men from both sides went to the same area, the farmlands around Dranesville, looking for food and hay. In the early morning of the 20th, the two armies stumbled upon each other and artillery fires were exchanged until about 3 o'clock that afternoon. Five Pennsylvania Infantry Regiments from Camp Pierport under Brig. Gen. Ord suffered a loss of 68 men. The Confederate Brig. Gen. Stuart lost 194 men. (source #25)

3. The most common Civil War small arms ammunition was the dreadful Minnie ball, which tore an enormous wound on impact. Of the approximate 175,000 wounds to the extremities received among the Federal troops, about 30,000 led to amputation. Contrary to popular myth, most amputees did not experience surgery without anesthetic. Ample doses of chloroform were administered. Those who survived

the surgery had another hurdle, the high risk of infection. Although most surgeons were aware of the connection between cleanliness and low infection rates, they did not know how to sterilize their equipment. Due to frequent water shortage, surgeons often went days without washing their hands or instruments. The resulting infections, known as "surgical fever," were common after surgery. Despite these fearful odds, nearly 75 percent of the amputees survived. (source #18)

4. Of all the unusual combat units of the Civil War, none was more colorful than the Pennsylvania Bucktails (13th Pennsylvania Reserve). In the spring of 1861, there came from the mountains of Pennsylvania's "Wildcat District" a group of young men who would form the nucleus of a regiment destined to become famous. The regiment was made up mostly of rough and hardy lumberjacks who had their own peculiar "wildcat yell." Because of the regiment's custom of having each man wear on his hat the tail of a deer he had shot, the 13th Pennsylvania became known as the "Bucktails."

The Bucktails were all superior marksmen, and during the first year of the war, they distinguished themselves as skirmishers and sharpshooters. Companies of the 13th were in the hot spots of the major battles: Dranesville, Seven Days Retreat-Mechanicsville, Gaines' Mill, Savage Station,

White Oak Swamp, and Malvern Hill, the second battle of Bull Run, Antietam, Fredericksburg, Gettysburg, Battles of the Wilderness, Spotsylvania, and Bethesda Church. They mustered out in June of 1864 having lost over half of their original number. An interesting side note: Bucktails from Company F of the 150th were assigned to the Soldier's Home (the Lincoln's summer White House) as bodyguards for President Lincoln. They continued this duty until his assassination. (source #26)

5   saleratus: Baking powder as we know it today had not yet been invented, and the product they used instead, known as "saleratus," tasted pretty nasty. (source #27)

Main Street, Looking West, Everett, PA

Courtesy of Barbara Miller

The Letters

1862

CAMP PIERPONT, VIRGINIA
JANUARY 3, 1862

Dear Father,

Christmas passed very pleasantly in camp. Nothing of importance occurred in our Regiment. But thanks to our dear kind friends at home, and the good things sent to us, we had a most excellent dinner and enjoyed it exceedingly. Please accept my humble, grateful acknowledgement.

I have got[ten] to be a great cook and can get up a meal fit for any soldier or civilian to eat. My greatest success in cooking consists in baking cakes. I get flour and corn meal about equal portions, stir them up in water, add a little salt and 3 or 4 eggs, and then bake them in the form of flannel cakes.[1] I think I can beat any woman baking these cakes that I ever saw try. Several who have eaten them say they never eat better at home.

New Year's Day we spent on picket. Companies A and F were the 2 out. The weather was delightful and we had a very pleasant time. Nothing of importance occurred. I had not anything at all to do. Spent my time in reading, smoking, talking, etc., and had an easy time of it. Well, another year has gone and is recorded with the past; an eventful year, truly giving birth to the most unholy and wicked rebellion ever known.[2] What the year just born may accomplish Heaven alone can now tell. God grant it may restore peace and prosperity to our land, but ere this is done, many valuable lives and brave hearts must be quenched in death. Oh, what an awful account the leaders of the rebellion will have to answer before God.

There is a good deal of speculation here relative to the interference or non-interference of England.[3] Ambition seems to urge her to shake the lion's paw, but if she does, I doubt not, it will get caught in a trap, and it will at least lose some of its toes if she saves her crown. But I pray she may let us alone, for her interference would cost a vast amount of blood.

We have had no really cold weather yet. No snow. It is sleeting a little this evening. We are getting along finely. Lizzie's letter came last night. Much love to all.

Your Affectionate Son,

James

I will write Bro. Moore in a day or two. I think we will receive our pay in a week or so.

Author's Notes

1. **Flannel cakes**

   1 qt. milk

   3 tbs. [homemade] yeast

   1 tbs. butter, melted

   2 eggs, well beaten

   1 tsp. salt

   Flour

   [Mix the milk, yeast, and salt, then add enough] Flour
   to make a good batter. Set the rest of the ingredients as a
   sponge overnight, and in the morning add the melted butter
   and eggs.

   This recipe was found in the book *Common Sense in the
   Household* by Marian Harland (New York, 1871). Mrs.
   Harland was more cryptic than usual with directions here,
   so the parts in brackets were added for clarification. Like
   many recipes of the time for breakfast breads—essentially
   pancakes—a careful balance had to be found. This recipe
   uses a small amount of yeast relative to the quantity of other
   ingredients, since it was to be left out overnight to save the

cook a bit of time in the morning. That amount of yeast would induce just enough rising to make the dough light, without causing such an expansion as to engulf half the kitchen. If you try this today, place the batter overnight in the coolest part of the room; do not refrigerate it as this will keep the yeast from functioning at all. If homemade yeast is not available, try to find the moist cake form of the product rather than the dry powder in packets. (source #27)

2. As James looked back at the year gone by, and looked ahead at what the year just born might bring, it appears that his need for reflection was shared by General "Stonewall" Jackson as he wrote to his wife, Mary Anna, on December 25, 1862: "But what a cruel thing is war; to separate and destroy families and friends, and mar the purest joy and happiness God has granted us in this world; to fill our hearts with hatred instead of love for our neighbors, and to devastate the fair face of this beautiful world." (source #61, p. 167)

3. "Cotton is King!" Anonymous. This was a popular expression in the South. (source #61, p. 15)

Most Southerners hoped that cotton would provide the leverage they needed to induce England and France to side with the Confederacy. The Confederate Congress did not officially declare an embargo, but state governments and

private citizens created a shortage by withholding cotton
from the market. Their hope was that this action would
adversely affect the European mills, encouraging them
to give military aid to the Confederacy or disregard the
Union blockades. But the "King Cotton" strategy had three
major flaws. First, a bumper crop in 1860 had allowed the
European mills to build up their own stock. The effect of the
embargo was not felt until late 1862, and by 1863 cotton
imported from India, Egypt, and Brazil resolved the cotton
shortage in Europe. Second, the Confederacy did not consider how strongly Europe feared the possibility of engaging
in war with the U. S. Finally, the cotton industry in the South
relied heavily on slavery, and England was the worldwide
leader in the abolitionist movement. England's position of
neutrality became stronger after the Southern armies suffered reversals beginning with Gettysburg. Jefferson Davis,
the president of the Confederacy, realized too late that their
strategy had failed, and they lost their chance to use their
strongest asset to finance the war. (source #28)

"Can any sane man believe that England and France will
consent, as is now suggested, to stultify the policy of half a
century for the sake of an extended cotton trade, and to purchase the favors of Charleston and Milledgeville by recog-
nizing what has been called the isothermal law, which impels
African labor toward the tropics on the other side of the

Atlantic?"—Editorial, *Times* (London), November 29, 1860.
The London newspaper was ridiculing the Southern hope
that England and France would support the Confederacy in
order to save cotton supplies. (source #61, p. 84)

Camp Piermont, Va
January 10, 1862

Dear Father,

I received a letter from Lizzie a day or two ago in which she stated that you were not very well. I do hope you are by this time better. Please write me and let me know, for whenever you are unwell I feel very uneasy, fearing something serious may be the matter. I pray God may preserve you and grant you many years of health and usefulness. My health continues excellent. John Barmond is still in the hospital. I was in to see him this morning. He is in good spirits, but his leg is quite bad and it will be a good while before he returns to duty.

Our company is getting small owing to the 4 deaths and 4 men detailed for detached service.[1] If you can learn of any young men who would like to enlist, please send me their names. They would have a much better time to join now than we had. When we joined for service, we had to go into camp and lie a long time without clothing or anything else to keep us comfortable. Anyone joining now receives uniforms and equipment immediately. Indeed this is the very best time a man could enlist. You are around a good deal and might hear of 5 or 6 who would like to lend a helping hand in the cause. Ask Jacob Williams if he knows of any.

The weather here is now warm but damp, and the ground is muddy, which makes tramping around very laborious and disagreeable.

We have not yet received our pay, but expect to in a few days. Privates pay is $13.00, Sergeants $17.00, 1st Sergeants $20.00.[2] All get $100 at the end of the war and most likely bounty land of 160 acres. If disabled, a pension of $8.00 per month.

Capt. has returned and looks well. Thomas Williams from Clearfield was here to see me yesterday. He says Dr. Bunn is doing finely. Has not drank any for more than a year, keeps two horses, is riding constantly, and is building a large house and barn. Capt. Dowler is with a company in Washington. Remember me to all. In much love, I am

Your Affectionate Son,

Jamie

year. Keps two horses. is riding
Constantly and is building a
large house and bar d.
Capt Dowler is with a Company
in Washington.
  Remember me to all
    in much love I am
      Your Affectionate Sen

        James

The final page of James's January 10, 1862, letter

Author's Notes

1. Detached service, meaning the temporary transfer of a soldier to another unit or assignment. (source #64)

2. The pay schedule is per month.

Camp Pierpont, Va.
January 30, 1862

Dear Father,

Enclosed please find ten dolls. As soon as you receive it please let me know and I will send more. I do not like to send much at a time for fear it may be lost and never reach you.

My boils are getting better, but I am still unable to run around much and am unfit for duty. I was confined to my bed with them for two weeks, but have been able to get about through the quarters a little yesterday and to-day, and I can assure you it is quite cheering to get out again among the boys. Even though I cannot engage in any of their sports, it does me good to look at them. I have two boils on my right forearm. They broke to-day and are now easy. I do not know how many I have on my legs and other parts of my body, but enough at any rate to make me feel pretty bad and keep me in bed. They are, however, nearly all broken now and I think will leave me. You can hardly imagine how glad I feel. I do not know what made them come out so on me. I am sure it was not eating fat meat, for that I never touch, only to fry the grease out to burn in an oil tin box which we use as a lamp. It makes an excellent light and saves many candles for which, when we buy, we have to pay 5 cents a piece.

The M.D.s tell us that every boil is worth 5 dolls, but I would have most willingly sold out at half price. I suppose you think by this time that this is rather a boiling letter, and I must change the subject. The general health of the company remains good. One only, John Barmond, being in the hospital.

The weather continues warm but wet and disagreeable, mud quite deep. I am glad your prospects on the circuit are so cheering and pray God he may bless all your labors. Rest indeed cannot be found in this earthly state. But I hope we may all rest together through vast Eternity at the right hand of the Father. I often think it matters so little what we are here, whether rich or poor, honored or obscure, that it is not worth a thought so that we honor God, do all His will concerning us, and are prepared to reign with Him forever. Time is so very, very short and Eternity so inconceivable long. Dear Father, I have never regretted the steps I took on the 23rd of April 1861. I have no doubts about being in the path of duty and believe I can consistently ask the blessing of Heaven on my work even though I may have to take the lives of my fellow men, the right to which they have forfeited by breaking the law and committing murder in a twofold sense.

I understand Samuel Williams has embraced religion. Tell him to hold fast, shun even the appearance of evil, and go on to perfection. Remember me in much love to Mother and to the friends at the Run and to Mr. Ashcum and family.

Truly Your Affectionate Son,

Jamie

I sent a letter to Bedford Inquirer today.

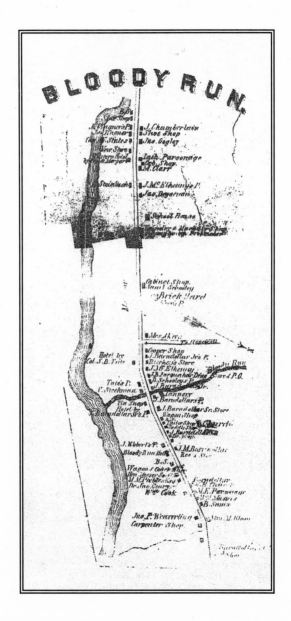

Bloody Run map courtesy of Bedford County Historical Society

The following is the letter that James wrote to the Bedford Inquirer. *It was printed February 14, 1862, under the heading "LETTERS FROM OUR SOLDIERS."* [1]

CAMP PIERPONT, VA.
JANUARY, 1862

Mr. Editor:

Dear Sir: We are glad to learn that old Bedford County has furnished so many companies for the three years' service and so nobly given many of her young men to the country in the hour of need, to battle for our civil and religious liberties, the union of the States, and the Constitution and Laws as they were bequeathed us by the Patriot Sires of '76. We pray Heaven she may have her reward in seeing rebellion soon crushed, the union restored, and every section, every State united in one eternal brotherhood, never again to be broken or rent. Then shall treason hide its accursed head in the dust and our native Eagle shall rise—soaring high in the heavens, flap his wings for joy and bear messages of freedom, peace, and good will, from the Northern lakes to the Southern gulf, and from the Atlantic to the Pacific, and all the nations of the earth shall do us honor and call us thrice blessed.

Before this shall be accomplished, Slavery, the cornerstone of the Southern Aristocracy, may, and we hope, will have to be blotted, as a curse, from our land and the U. S. A., with all the boasted power of the Cotton King, and God, made our vast wilderness. But then and not till then shall many of Bedford's sons return to honor her, as she has honored her country in the trying hour. In the meantime, we pledge ourselves she shall not have cause to mourn her children's shame or blush for them in the day of battle; yet we are sorry she still has some young men at home who could well join us in the struggle. There are yet, however, young men needed to fill up the different companies, and they may yet win the esteem of good and loyal men by joining heart and hand with us.

Now for our company, formerly known as the "Hopewell Rifles," but now Company F, Eighth Regiment P. V., and attached to the 1st or Gen. Reynolds brigade. It is doubtless well known to most of your readers that we went into Camp Wilkins, at Pittsburgh, June 11, 1861, in which we remained as a camp of instruction until, at a call from the President, July 1st, we moved to Washington and have since changed station three times, doing in the meantime much and probably important labor such as picket duty, working on fortification, etc., but no fighting at which the men have murmured not a little.

We are now encamped near the Washington and Leesburg road, 8 miles from Washington and 12 from Dranesville, in the direction of which we make all our scouting and foraging expeditions. We have several times penetrated the enemy's lines, driving in their pickets, and once advanced beyond Dranesville, but though those excursions always pay well, in Secesh[2] corn, hay, oats, etc., we have never been fortunate or unfortunate enough to meet the enemy in battle. They [James's fellow soldiers] don't seem to like this. They say, "We came to fight and we want to do it," but they begin to think the rebels know the country, and understand running too well to meet us this side of Manassas, Centerville, or Leesburg. The time for us to advance there seems in the minds of the rulers to be not yet. God grant them the wisdom to know.

In camp we have but little now to do save guard duty. The ground, owing to the late heavy rains, being so soft and muddy that drilling is almost impossible. We spent our time mostly in the tents reading, writing, social conversation, etc., or when the weather will permit, in outdoor athletic exercise, and in this we practice all the games ingenuity can invent or recollection bring to mind including foot racing, jumping, football, boxing, etc. In the use of the gloves, sometimes a knockdown or a bloody nose is given and received, but even this passes off pleasantly, no one presuming to get angry or at least not to show it, for in this case he would be severely hooted at and become the butt of the company, not a desirable position. A great many dry and some practical jokes are also practiced. They also pass off pleasantly. We have not had a fight in the company since coming to camp, which I venture there are few companies in the Brigade can say.

We have lost 4 members by disease, but the health of the men is now good, but one man is in the hospital, and he is getting well. Reading matter is devoured with avidity. Thousands of newspapers are daily sold in the camps, and there is but little danger of the army becoming deficient in general intelligence so essential for a Republican people.

This is already extended to a much greater length than we had intended, so with best wishes to all friends we will close.

Yours,
J. Cleaver

Author's Notes

1. This letter was retrieved from microfilm at the Pioneer Library of the Bedford County Historical Society.

2. "Secesh" was short for secession or secessionist.

The news of the last week has been most cheering indeed to us. but no doubt disheartening in the extreme to the rebels. I rather suppose. Their favorite theory. viz. That "One Southron is as good as five Yankee" is about played out by this time.

It is to be hoped that Newspaper Editors. and designing politicians who have been murmuring at. and in a measure tying the hands of Gen. McClellan. will now have some thing to engage their attention. without dwelling So much on that eternal "Onward To Richmond." We would all like very well to take Manassas and move on to Richmond &c I doubt not we could have done it months ago. but not without a loss of 2 0. or 30. thousand men. And it would not be worth

The second page of James's February 20, 1862, letter
(also the letter featured on the cover)

CAMP PIERPONT, VA.
FEBRUARY 20, 1862

Dear Father,

I have not written you for several days nor have I felt like writing. I have been suffering a great deal from these boils. A very sore one on the back of my hand is just open and is easier than it has been.

I received a letter from Lizzie last night in which she says you have not heard from me for some time and that you feel uneasy. I answered your last immediately after receiving it and enclosed ten dolls and have not yet heard from it. Did you receive a second $10.00 bill since pay day? Please let me know soon.

The news of the last week has been most cheering indeed to us but no doubt disheartening in the extreme to the rebels, I rather suppose. Their favorite theory that "One Southern is as good as five Yanks" is about played out by this time.

It is to be hoped that newspaper editors and designing politicians who have been murmuring at and in a measure tying the hands of Gen. McClellan will now have something to engage their attention without dwelling so much on that eternal "Onward to Richmond." We would all like very well to take Manassas and move on to Richmond, and I doubt not we could have done it months ago, but not without a loss of 20 or 30 thousand men and it would not be worth half that to us if we had. And it never has been the policy of a good general to move an army on to the strongest fortification an enemy has until he has weakened them all he can. The rebel forces are daily being drawn off from Manassas to protect more important places.

We have orders to pack up such clothing as we do not need so as to be ready to send them to Washington, which seems to indicate a move as soon as the state of the roads will permit. The men seem tired of lying in camp and marching orders now would be hailed with joy. We would like to take Leesburg and avenge the death of Gen. Baker.[1] Gen. Stone's[2] arrest gives the greatest satisfaction here and inspires us with fresh confidence in our officers and rulers. God grant they may prove themselves worthy of confidence reposed in them.

How do things look about the Run? I suppose there is but little excitement there now. People marry and are given in marriage as usual, so I learn. How does Dinah stand running this winter? Are there any improvements going on at the Run? Remember me to all the friends.

With love to yourself and Mother,

I am your son,

Jamie

Feb. 22. Company out on picket. Raining. Ground and roads very muddy. Does not look like moving for some time. I am getting better. This morning a strong force of our cavalry went out to drive in the enemy's pickets. Have not heard from them. Received a letter from Bro. Brian. He is well.

Author's Notes

1. General Edward Baker (1811–1861) was an English-born
   American politician, lawyer, and military leader. Baker served
   as U. S. Army colonel during both the Mexican-American
   War and the American Civil War. He was a sitting U. S.
   senator and close friend of President Lincoln. Baker had
   recently been offered a commission as major general of the
   volunteers. He was deciding whether to leave the Senate
   to accept this commission. McClellan had recently been
   made general-in-chief of all Union Armies. He chose to
   launch a reconnaissance in hopes of seizing Potomac River
   crossing sites and ultimately Leesburg, Virginia. McClellan
   ordered Brigadier General Stone to stage a distraction at
   Edward's Ferry. Stone wanted a second distraction up the
   river and gave this task to Colonel Edward Baker. Stone's
   written instructions to Baker ordered that additional forces
   under Baker's command were to cross to the Virginia side,
   or to be completely withdrawn at Baker's discretion. Instead
   of crossing to the bluff personally to evaluate his tactical
   options, Colonel Baker immediately chose to cross his entire
   force, and for some hours personally supervised the lifting of

boats from the nearby Chesapeake and Ohio Canal to assist his river crossing. During the undertaking of this mission, Colonel Baker was shot. Many of the Union soldiers were driven over the steep bluff and into the river. Boats attempting to cross back to Harrison Island were soon swamped and capsized; a disturbing number of the casualties resulted from drowning. More than 500 Union prisoners were captured on the banks of the Potomac later that night.

This Union defeat was relatively minor in comparison to the battles to come in the war, but it had an enormous impact. The loss of a sitting senator had severe political ramifications in Washington. General Stone was treated as the scapegoat for the defeat. (source #29)

2. General Charles Stone (1824–1887), a West Point graduate in 1845, was a career United States Army officer, civil engineer, and surveyor. He fought with distinction in the Mexican-American War. Stone was requested to be Inspector General of the District of Columbia Militia at the rank of colonel as of January 1, 1861, thus becoming the first volunteer officer mustered into the Union Army before the Civil War. In this role, he secured the capital for the arrival of President-elect Abraham Lincoln, and was personally responsible for security at the new president's inaugural. By August of that year, Stone was appointed brigadier general of

volunteers. In October 1861, he sent a portion of his command to attack a suspected Confederate camp near Leesburg, Virginia, and was soundly defeated at the Battle of Ball's Bluff. It was here that his subordinate, Colonel Baker, was killed in battle. Stone bore the brunt of much public criticism. Suspected of disloyalty and treason, Stone was arrested on February 9, 1862, on orders of Major General McClellan who was acting under orders from Secretary of War Edwin M. Stanton. No charges were ever filed against Stone, but he was confined for 189 days in Fort Lafayette and later Fort Hamilton. Stone was released without explanation or apology on August 16, 1862. Stone served in several other assignments until Stanton ordered Stone to muster out of his volunteer commission as a brigadier general and Stone was reverted to his rank of colonel in the regular army. Stone resigned from the army in September 1864, before the end of the war. (source #30)

Camp Pierpont, Va.
February 22, 1862

Dear Father,

The enclosed dated on the 20th I had written the day before yesterday but neglected sending it away this morning. This evening I received yours of the 18th. And as it always does, it gave me the greatest pleasure to learn that you are all well. I was going to say, you do not know how anxious I always am to hear from you, but you I know can judge of my anxiety for your welfare by yours for mine, which I'm sure is great. I often think that paternal, maternal, and filial affection are the strongest ties that can bind hearts together and nothing but a strong sense of duty could have induced me to have left home. And no one knows what a solace it is to me to feel assured that I have your blessing. Every sentence in your letters assuring me that you feel and believe me to be in the right path of duty and in a righteous and holy cause is as a star of hope to my heart bringing sunshine and joy where otherwise would be darkness and gloom.

You speak of that Inquirer letter. I have seen it in print and am ashamed of it. Not however of the Abolition sentiment you say some complain of it, but the whole style of it. It was written one day while lying in bed suffering a good deal of pain. As for the abolitionism, when I left home I was no more of an abolitionist than anyone else. But my heart is <u>All American</u> and every pulsation beats and every drop of blood therein flows for our republican institutions. When I see what ruin, <u>Slavery</u>, that more than demigod of the Southern Aristocracy, has wrought; when I consider how it has fought against the Constitution, and even aimed its blow at everything tending to benevolence, philanthropy, enlightenment, or Patriotism and how it is now pampered and cherished by many even among Northern men who would even now save slavery at the expense of the Union, <u>I say with my whole heart, Death to its root and branch.</u> I am a Jim Lane man. I do not want to see this war fought over again in ten or fifteen years, but I wish to have the questions of our Union settled now forever.

Do not, however, understand me to say I would have slavery crushed by other than Constitutional measures, not by any means, for I would fight by the side of a slave holder if he were on the side of the Constitution. But I go in for putting down rebellion and while we are doing this, let slavery take care of itself and like the negroes' [illegible, possibly "cheer"], "It will soon kill itself"—perhaps long before we can kill [the] rebellion, but at the furthest I hope they will fall together. But enough of this, I do not intend writing for newspapers soon again. I rather think I can save my credit a great deal better by keeping <u>Mum</u>. I hope this may reach you before you start for conference. If so, please answer it at your earliest convenience.

I long for you to pay us a visit and look forward to the time when I shall see you with fond anticipation. Please bring me if you possibly can a pint or half-pint of your clothes cleaning mixture, a little of homemade salve, and some needles. If you can get me a pound or two of tobacco in Baltimore, I will pay you for it. We've very inferior article [tobacco] here and have to pay an enormous price for it. With much love to Mother and kin, Regards to all the friends,

Your Affectionate Son,

Jamie

Barndollar Methodist Episcopal Church courtesy of Barbara Miller

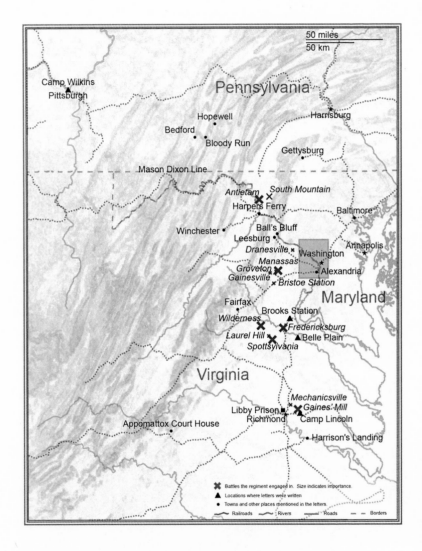

Map of James's locations throughout the Civil War

Custom Civil War maps designed by John C. Nelson

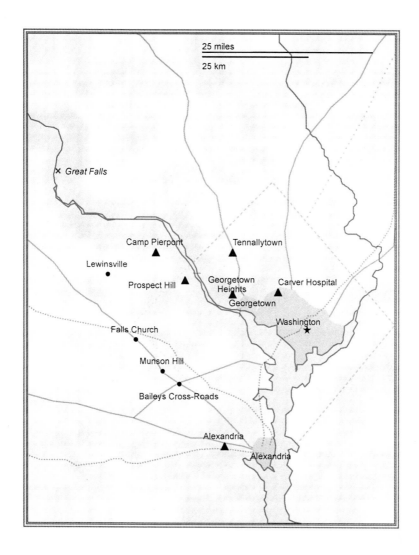

A closer look at the Washington, D. C., region

http://www.civilwarhistorymaps.com

CAMP PIERPONT, VA
MARCH 3, 1862

Dear Father,

I presume today you are in Baltimore and I wish I were with you, but that is out of the question. Rev. Consor tried hard to get a leave of absence to attend the conference, but failed. You have doubtless read my letters directed to Baltimore. Written at a time we expected to move immediately, but that excitement has now died away. Although of course we cannot tell, we do not expect to move for some time, and I think yourself and John would be safe in paying us a visit. We are in McCall's Division near Langley. When you get there, anyone will inform you where the 8th Penna Reserve is encamped. From Washington you can take a streetcar or omnibus to Georgetown. There you can take the stage to Langley. At what time I am unable to say, but you can easily learn by inquiry, <u>sometime in the forenoon</u>.

To-day we took a march to chain bridges with knapsacks on to accustom ourselves to marching preparatory to the spring and summer work. I am getting quite stout again and stood the tramp much better than I had expected. The roads remain quite muddy and to-night it is raining fast. I pity the companies that are out on picket.

Remember me to my friends in Baltimore. I should be happy to hear from any of them. I wrote to Uncle John some time ago but received no answer. Remember me to him and Uncle Daniel and their families if you see them. Tell them I like the army and feel ready to meet Jeff Davis. You find things in Baltimore materially changed since your last visit there and Union men are not now afraid to speak their sentiments openly.

Tell John to write to me. I need not write you both at the same time. Please answer this at your earliest convenience. I have been very busy making out Muster Rolls, etc.[1]

Your Affectionate Son,

James

<u>Do come out</u>. When I see you I will have much to talk about.

Author's Note

1. A muster roll is an inventory or roster, specifically a register of the officers and men in a military unit. (source #42)

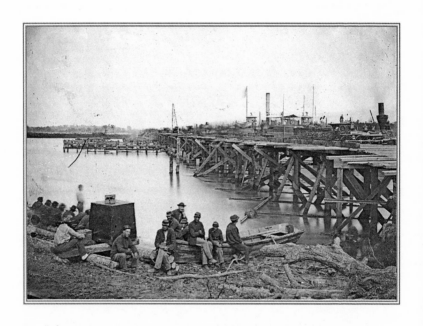

Bridge across Pamunkey River, Va, at White House Landing

Courtesy of National Archives, photo no. 111-B-2731
(Brady Collection)

On March 10, 1862, the entire division moved from Camp Pierpont to Hunter's Hill, Virginia, with the idea that they would join a general advance of the army on the Confederate position at Manassas. However, it was found that the enemy had evacuated its line of defenses. The plan of the campaign was changed by the commanding general, McClelland, and the reserve regiments were ordered back to the Potomac. On the 12th, the division marched through mud, darkness, and a deluge of rain to Alexandria with the intent of joining the Army of the Potomac. Instead, McCall's division was assigned to duty with the 1st corps, under General McDowell, which was held between the Potomac and the Rappahannock rivers for the protection of Washington.

From Alexandria, the 8th, with its brigade, marched back to Manassas, Warrenton Junction, and Falmouth. By May 24, they crossed the Rappahannock to Fredericksburg, Va. where General Reynolds was appointed military governor. An advance from Fredericksburg along the railroad toward Richmond was planned, but ultimately determined to be inexpedient. Since McClellan had put out an urgent call for reinforcements, Reynolds's brigade was recalled from its position at the railroad. The whole division marched to Gray's Landing and embarked for White House on the Pamunkey River, where they arrived on June 11. The Union Army had a vast store of supplies there and the timely arrival of the reserves prevented the destruction of these stores by a strong detachment of Confederate cavalry under Lee, who was on his way to Pamunkey for that very purpose. (source #1, p. 119; #2, p. 757)

Libby Prison, Richmond, Va., April 1865

Courtesy of National Archives, photographed by Alexander Gardner,
photo no. 165-SB-89

CAMP OPPOSITE FREDRICKSBURG, VA MAY 5, 1862

Dear Father,

Yours of April 30th was received last evening and it really did my heart good as it always does to receive a letter from you or anyone at home.

It is strange you did not receive a letter I wrote from Manassas and equally strange that John has received no letter from me since conference as I have written him several times. You can learn what section of the country I am in at any time by remembering that I am in McDowell's Corp, McClellan's Division, and General Reynold's on 1st Brigade. We are now just opposite Fredricksburg, the Rappahannock being between it and us. Troops are daily coming in, but I know not when we will move onward. I suppose the Yorktown fight will determine this in a measure.

We are encamped in a beautiful tract of woodland and have the prettiest camp we have had yet. The weather is mild and delightfully pleasant, and we enjoy ourselves just about as well as it is possible for soldiers to do. The orders are not very stringent and we move about nearly as much as we please so that we keep within the picket line and I suppose it would hardly [be] safe for one or two men to get outside. There are plenty of secessionists in these parts. Some of them I doubt not have been in the Rebel service, but since our advance have exchanged the Davis uniform for the garb of peaceable citizens. But are still ready to do what they can safely [do] in the unholy cause.

Yesterday was Sunday and was to me the most profitable day I have spent for a long time. We had preaching at 11 A.M. and despairing of our chaplains doing anything for our spiritual interest, we have formed a class—pray meetings and Bible class—independent of him. And from present appearance we hope for success through the blessing of God. The cause of religion in the Regiment for a long time has looked dark indeed and I fear the love of many has waxed cold, but I hope the Lord will in his mercy revive his work among us. I fear our chaplain instead of being a holy man of God doing continually his Master's work has been an offence and stumbling block to many. J. B. Linn is one of the most active and conscientious Christians in the Regiment.

The health of the company is good. John Barmond has got home but has to walk on crutches from his sore leg, which he cut in the winter. The names of the Bedford Co. boys killed at Winchester are John Ferguson, William College, and Phillip Croft[1] all from near Yellow Creek. Harry Kay[2] is said to have acted bravely.

He fired 12 shots from his carbine and then rushing in with sword and pistol took one prisoner.

I received the salve. I do not need it at present, but will keep it. It may be useful. My health never was better. I weigh about 160, wear whiskers full length and short hair, but I think I will soon cut my whiskers off. Remember me to Mother and Lizzie. Write soon.

Your Very Affectionate Son,

Jamie

Author's Notes

1. PA 110th Regiment, Company C (source #2, Vol. III, p. 993; #54; #55)

   John Ferguson, Private, mustered in 10/24/61; killed in action at Winchester, Virginia, 3/23/62

   John William College, Private, mustered in 10/24/61; died on 3/24/62 from wounds received at Winchester, Virginia, 3/23/62

   Phillip P. Croft, Private, mustered in 10/24/61; promoted to Corporal; killed in action at Winchester, Virginia, 3/23/62

2. Company F soldier: (source #1, p. 122; #2, p. 775; #54; #55)

   Wm. Harry Kay, Private, mustered in 6/19/61; died 9/18/62 of wounds received at South Mountain, 9/14/62

The following letter to his brother John was written five days before James was captured.

Camp Lincoln Right Wing Army Before Richmond, June 21, 1862

Dear Brother,

Yours of the 12th is at hand this morning and although I wrote yesterday, I will embrace this early opportunity of answering. I have no doubt as you say that you were "all startled at the seeming reverse of Banks." But I am surprised that anyone should for a moment have supposed Washington in danger. Why, before Jackson could have got[ten] there, he would have had to have marched over a hecatomb [100 tombs] of dead men, free men, of Banks', Fremont's, and McDowell's corps.[1] Jackson[2] is doubtless a good officer especially in the mountainous districts where he is well acquainted, but he is near our Capital now as he will likely be except in irons. I am glad, however, that your lot is among Patriots ready to fly at a moment to avert danger from our Country.

The enemy have indeed acted cruelly, nay, brutally toward the defenseless sympathizers of their Country. But strangest of all, the she Rebels have thrown aside every claim to the title of women and are worse than the men. However, as our army moves gradually on and our cause is understood, our leniency is becoming more appreciated and acts of barbarity are growing more rare. I often think our Government is too lenient and shows mercy at the expense of justice but perhaps this is the true Christian course.

I know you are all looking with an anxious eye toward Richmond. But do not grow impatient. You can form no idea of what a vast amount of labor is being done here. Newspaper sketches are all imperfect or at least quickly gotten up pictures. I could not I know give you any idea of things here and shall not attempt it. More than that, two great armies are standing in the very face of each other, one offensive and the other defensive. And all the preparations for attack and defense that great minds can conceive are being made. McClellan will not, I am sure, move before he is ready and his movements will now necessarily have to be slow and cautious. He is getting large-size guns constantly and Richmond is doomed. McClellan is a great general but best of all he is a man of God and puts his trust in the Most High.

Prof. Lowe's balloon goes up just in rear of our camp.[3] Yesterday, Secesh, not liking such close watching, sent a shell screaming at him, but it fell short and exploded without doing any harm.

Tell me what papers you get. Jacob B. Linn is in our company. Is a first-rate fellow and getting along finely. His health has always been good.

Your most affect[ionate],

Brother *Jamie*

Do write often.

Author's Notes

1. Just before the war, Nathaniel Banks (1816–1894) was serving as governor of Massachusetts. He was named a major general of the volunteers. With no prior military experience, he was in the divisional and departmental command near Washington early in the war. His war record was dismal and for a while was without a command. He mustered out in 1865 and continued his political career in Congress, the state senate, and as a U. S. marshal. (source #9)

John Fremont (1813–1890), one of four major generals appointed by President Lincoln, was the most celebrated. His major Civil War contributions were more political than military for he focused Union attention on the role that emancipation should play in the North's war policy. Fremont endured several crushing losses against "Stonewall" Jackson during the general's brilliantly successful Shenandoah Valley campaign. After a military reorganization placed him under the command of former subordinate John Pope, Fremont angrily resigned his post, never to receive a new Civil War appointment. (source #9)

General Irwin Mc Dowell (1818–1885) was an Ohio native who graduated from West Point in 1838. He was assigned to command the troops around the capital. Political pressure made it necessary for McDowell to advance on Manassas before his troops were ready. While his plan had merit, it was too much for the raw volunteers to accomplish. He was head of the 1st Corps of the Army of the Potomac, which was left behind to guard the approaches to Washington while McClellan moved to the Peninsula. He was supposed to march overland to join McClellan, but the activities of Stonewall Jackson in the Shenandoah Valley precluded this maneuver. McDowell mustered out of the volunteers in 1866, became a major general in the regular establishment six years later, and retired in 1882. (source #9)

2. Next to Robert E. Lee, Thomas Jonathan "Stonewall" Jackson (1824–1863) was the most revered of all the Confederate commanders. He graduated from West Point in 1846, served in the Mexican War, and resigned to accept a professorship at Virginia Military Institute. In the fight at the First Bull Run, the brigade and its commander distinguished themselves to such a degree that they were dubbed "Stonewall" by General Barnard Bee. At a low point in the battle, Bee was encouraged by Jackson who spoke with a blazing and defiant look. His bold and prompt determination sent Bee back to his men with new life. Bee excitedly shouted, "Let us determine

to die here, and we will conquer. There is Jackson standing like a stone wall. Rally behind the Virginians!" A number of Bee's men rallied and followed him in a charge against the advancing enemy, in which this heroic leader was killed. The 1st Brigade became known as the Stonewall brigade and was the only Confederate brigade to have a nickname become its official designation. (source #9, #10)

Some day the men of that brigade will be proud to say to their children, "I was one of the Stonewall Brigade." Quoted by Lieut. Col. G. F. R. Henderson in *Stonewall Jackson and the American Civil War*, vol. 2, 1898. Jackson considered that the name "Stonewall" belonged to the brigade and not personally to himself. (source #61, p. 172)

On his greatest day, May 2, 1863, Jackson led his corps around the Union right flank at Chancellorsville. While out on reconnaissance that night, Jackson was mortally wounded by some of his own men as he was returning to his own lines. Following the amputation of his arm, he died eight days later from pneumonia. (sources #9, #10)

"I consider these wounds a blessing; they were given me for some good and wise purpose, and I would not part with them if I could." Quoted by John Estern Cooke in *The Life of Stonewall Jackson*, vol.1, 1863. Jackson said this as he lay dying. (source #61, p. 168)

3. The use of balloons for surveillance dates back to the 1700s, but the Civil War was the first war in which they were used for military purposes. In 1861, at the outbreak of the war, Lincoln appointed Thaddeus Lowe chief of army aeronautics. Lowe's first mission was to gather information on Confederate troops shortly after the First Bull Run in July 1861. On September 24, 1861, Lowe ascended to more than 1,000 feet near Arlington, Virginia. He began telegraphing intelligence on the Confederate troops located at Falls Church, Virginia, more than 3 miles away. Acting on this information, Union guns were aimed and fired accurately at Confederate troops without actually being able to see them. This was a first in the history of warfare.

    During McClellan's Peninsula Campaign, Lowe conducted almost daily flights over Virginia, producing reports and photographs of the Confederate positions. By the time he resigned his post in 1863, Lowe, along with his crew, had made more than three thousand flights over enemy territory. The balloon was attached to the earth by a strong but fine rope. It ascended from two to five hundred feet in the air and was hauled down when its aims had been fulfilled. An interesting side note: Prof. Lowe's granddaughter, Florence

"Pancho" Barnes, was one of the few female flyers and a contemporary of Amelia Earhart. A portion of her life is featured in the movie *The Right Stuff.* (source #31, "Balloons of the Army of the Potomac"; #9, #32, #38, October 26, 1861, issue of *Harper's Weekly*)

Battles of Mechanicsville: June 26, 1862
Battles of Gainesville: August 28, 1862
Battles of South Mountain: September 14, 1862
Antietam: September 16–17, 1862[1]

The regiment now moved to join the Army of the Potomac in the vicinity of Gaines' Mill. From there they took position at Mechanicsville and along the line of Beaver Dam. On June 26, 1862, the Battle of Mechanicsville was fought, the first in a series of bloody engagements known collectively as the Seven Days' Fight. With the exception of the skirmish at Dranesville in the previous December, this was the first engagement in which the 8th took part.

On the morning of June 26, at Mechanicsville, the 8th Reserve was to the left of the brigade line and about center on the line holding the bank of the Beaver Dam Creek. The battle began at about 3 o'clock P.M. The Georgia and Louisiana troops of the enemy waded the stream and gallantly rushed forward to attack. Three times the close columns of the enemy charged down the opposite slope with determined valor, but were always driven back. At night the men rested on the ground where they had fought. The dead were collected in blankets and consigned to the earth, and the wounded were sent to the rear.

Company F, being on the skirmish line and not comprehending the order to withdraw, remained at their post and fell into enemy hands. With regard to the capture of Company F, Lieutenant James Cleaver said that about two-thirds of the company were captured, he being one of the unfortunates, and that after having been marched into Richmond and detained for some six weeks, all captives were exchanged. According to the obituary of Capt. John Eichelberger, the captain and forty-one of his men were captured and taken to Libby prison in Richmond, Virginia, for 42 days.[2]

At dawn on the morning of June 27, the 8th and the companion regiments were withdrawn from the battleground and marched two or three miles to Gaines' Mill where they were placed in line of battle for a renewed conflict. McCall's Penna. 8th Reserves were placed in the second line. Approaching were soldiers of Generals A. P. Hill, Longstreet, D. H. Hill, and Jackson—in all, 50,000 against half that number on the Union side. The battle at Gaines' Mill ended in blood and defeat for the Union forces. At the end of the Seven Days' Fight, the loss of the 8th Reserve Regiment in killed, wounded, and missing was 230.

On August 11, the 8th moved to join General Pope. They took part in the Battles of Gainesville on August 28, Groveton on the 29th, and Bull Run on the 30th. They were attached to the Maryland Campaign from September 6–24, fighting in the Battles of South Mountain, Maryland, on September 14 and at Antietam on the 16th and 17th. They stayed in Maryland until October 30. They were on movement to Falmouth, Va, from October 30 to November 19.[3] (source #1, pp. 119-121; #2, pp. 757-761)

Authors Notes:

1. "We hope and pray that you may be permitted by a kind
    Providence, after the war is over, to return." Anonymous,
    quoted by Charles C. Coffin in *Century Magazine*, June
    1886. Coffin, a correspondent for the *Boston Journal*, found
    this inscription in a Bible resting on the chest of a dead
    Union soldier at the Battle of Antietam (Sharpsburg).
    (source #61, p. 9)

    "It was a dreadful scene. The dead and dying lay thick on
    the field like harvest sheaths.... Prayers were mingled with
    oaths, and midnight hid all distinction between blue and
    gray." From *I Rode with Stonewall*, by Henry Kyd Douglas,
    1940. Confederate Major Douglas was describing the after-
    math of the Battle of Antietam (Sharpsburg). His memoirs
    were published thirty-seven years after his death. (source
    #61, p. 81)

2. The following descriptions are from local Richmond
    newspapers in 1862 (source #57):

From the Richmond *Whig*, 6/28/1862

THE PRISONERS captured yesterday, and brought to the Libby prison were only thirty in number, and represent the following regiments: 7th Maine, 9th and 18th Mass., 10th, 25th and 43rd New York, 8th, 9th and 98th Pa., 1st Pa. Rifles, 1st and 4th Michigan. The only officer in the lot was a barefaced, barefooted Dutch Yankee. **Lieut. E. Eichelberger, of the 8th Pa.**, was captured by some means, in the vicinity of Seven Pines, yesterday morning.

From the Richmond *Dispatch*, 8/13/1862

Gone. – About one hundred and forty commissioned Federal officers, comprising those taken in the battles before Richmond, and those captured in the Valley, lately arrived from Lynchburg, were sent off yesterday, under an escort of 15 men, from Greanor's company, City Battalion, under Lieut. Hough. They started at 12 o'clock for Varina, twelve miles below Richmond. Eleven of the number who were unwell, and Gens. McCall, Reynolds, and Rankin went in wagons, which also served to convey the baggage of the party. One hundred and twenty-four of the officers started on foot. The day was excessively hot. On starting, only a few exhibited a truculent disposition. All seemed glad to be off, and sundry of them expressed the wish that the war might soon end.

3. For all five paragraphs: (source #1, pp. 119-121; #2, pp. 757-761)

The following letter, written three months after James's release from prison, suggests that he was back with his unit.

CAMP NEAR BROOK'S STATION, VA
NOVEMBER 25, 1862

Dear Brother,

Yours of the 18th is at hand last evening. I am surprised you do not receive my letters, for I have written frequently, but the interruption in the mails must be on account of our having been for some time in such out-of-the-way places. As long as we remain here, I think they will be more regular as we are near Aquia Creek and the cars are already on the road. We have had some longer trains since leaving Sharpsburg. In wet weather we have but little shelter and sometimes have to sit up by the fire all night, while it is raining, to keep ourselves warm as possible under the circumstances. But when it clears off we are again happy; build large fires, dry ourselves and blankets, and make up for lost sleep by sleeping the sounder. There is not much prospect of soon going into winter quarters and we expect it rough and hard this winter. But everyone so far seems willing to endure all so that it leads to the suppression of rebellion, for I can assure you there are none [who] wish to see the end of the war more than the soldier. The removal of McClellan[1] at first created a good deal of excitement and some dissatisfaction, especially in our Division for none loved little Mac more than the Penna Reserve. Some officers threatened to resign and some of the men swore they would not fight, but this was only childish simplicity for a good soldier, although he has his preferences, will nevertheless fight under any officer.

I at first feared it would make bad work and at the time would have laid down my life to prevent it, but I am happy to say all the excitement has calmed down and the men and officers are gaining confidence in Burnside every day.[2] Indeed, I have never seen the troops in better spirits. Burnside's plan of dividing his army into three Grand Divisions is certainly excellent and will enable us to move with much more promptness and rapidity, consequently with much more effect. Indeed, every act of Burnside so far shows him worthy of his position and makes everyone at least willing to give him a fair trial.

John, I am surprised at your assertion, "Horace is King."[3] You could not love McClellan more than I do and his removal could not wound you more. Yet I can see nothing in it to justify such an assertion. You know that inaction just at this time would be fatal to all our fondest hopes and give the enemy a greater advantage than they have ever had over us. McClelland refused to move. What then could be done but remove him.

I have heard a good many say, "It's an abolition move." How they can view it in that light I cannot see or how anyone can lay such a charge to the President, I cannot see. Is not Burnside [a Democrat] and has he not been a lifelong Democrat? Are not the majority of all the appointments given to Democrats? Was not Fremont an abolitionist? He was removed. Was not Hunter considered an abolitionist? He was removed. Aye, what was the cry against Simon Cameron[4] abolitionist? Was not Stanton[5] a Democrat appointed in his place? Lincoln's proclamation[6] did not make him an abolitionist in the common acceptance of the term. Have not rebels who have been 2 years in arms against their government a right to forfeit their property, niggers included? The southern army has been kept up by slave labor. Ought not the prop[erty] to be removed?

But enough of this. I am just such an abolitionist as Lincoln is. Indeed, I wish they would form the Negroes into Regiments, Brigades, and Divisions and put them to fighting their old masters. If we are not too good to be thrown into danger, the nigger is not. I am perfectly willing that a Negro should do my fighting. I do not care how black he may be.

Cannonading is just heard in the direction of Fredericksburg. I hope it is the bombarding of the town. For I know of no place I should love so much to see fall as that abominable city. If Burnside burns it, he will be the man among the soldiers.

Although some were opposed to filling up the Regiments with the drafted men, I believe it would be better for us than consolidation. The talk is of throwing the old companies and the Regiments of the reserve together and forming six full Regiments. If this be done, we lose our name as the 8th and <u>we have fought hard for it</u>. It will place the men under strange officers. And taking it that some must fall in every fight the consolidating plan would soon play the Reserve out and leave it known in name only as a thing that <u>did exist</u>. But I am worrying your patience and nearly freezing myself lying flat on my face a good way from the fire.

I am glad your wife enjoys herself so well and the people are so kind. Remember me in love to her.[7] I am going to write to her some of these days and you must not get jealous. Although I am comparatively but slightly acquainted with her, I will not have a sister and not write to her.

Maybe you think I have pleased a good many here in the last 3 or 4 lines.

Pray for us. I still have faith to believe that God will bless in His own good time.

Very Affectionately,
Your Brother

Jamie

Author's Notes

1. "In parting from you I cannot express the love and gratitude I bear to you. As an army you have grown up under my care. In you I have never found doubt or coldness. The battles you have fought under my command will proudly live in our nation's history.... Stand by General Burnside as you have stood by me and all will be well." —McClellan's farewell speech to the Army of the Potomac, November 7, 1862. He had been relieved of his command for failing to pursue General Robert E. Lee after the Battle of Antietam (Sharpsburg). (source #61, p. 309)

2. Ambrose Everett Burnside (1824–1881) was a West Point graduate in 1847. He was offered command of the main Union Army following McClellan's failure on the Peninsula. He refused this offer and several others that followed. He was then given charge of the 1st and 9th Corps during the Maryland operation. He fought at South Mountain and at Antietam. When McClellan was removed, Burnside was assigned to the command of the army. He hesitated, but was convinced that he had no alternative. His advance on

Fredericksburg was rapid, but later delays allowed Lee to easily repulse the Union attack. Burnside offered to retire, but this was refused. After the ill-fated Mud March, he was assigned to the department of Ohio. After other failures at Wilderness and Spotsylvania, he was sent on leave and never recalled. (source #9)

3. Horace Greeley (1811–1872) founded the *New York Tribune* in 1841 and was soon credited as one of the best journalists in New York City. Because the newspaper's readership was over one million, he could influence public opinion all over the nation. In the absence of other means of communication, the press had tremendous power. Greeley was a pioneer in the communication movement. (source #33)

4. Simon Cameron (1799–1889) was a politically powerful man during the mid nineteenth century in Pennsylvania and set the course of politics for nearly half a century. In 1817 he went to Harrisburg and although his career as a newspaper owner and editor was short, he became one of the leading Democratic journalists and most influential editors west of Philadelphia. He served in the Senate until 1849, when he was defeated. (source #34)

5. Edwin Stanton (1814–1869) was attorney general under President Buchanan and secretary of war under Abraham

Lincoln and Andrew Johnson. Stanton succeeded Simon Cameron in the Senate. (source #35)

6. The Emancipation Proclamation was an executive order issued by President Lincoln on January 1, 1863. It proclaimed the freedom of 3.1 million of the nation's 4 million slaves, and immediately freed 50,000 of them, with the rest freed as Union armies advanced. (source #65)

"On the first day of January in the year of our Lord, one thousand eight hundred and sixty-three, all persons held as slaves within any state, or designated part of a state, the people whereof shall then be in rebellion against the United States, shall be then, thenceforward, and forever free." —Lincoln's preliminary Emancipation Proclamation, September 22, 1862 (source #61, p. 245)

Two days later, President Lincoln gave the following response: "What I did, I did after very full deliberation, and under a heavy and solemn sense of responsibility. I can only trust in God that I have made no mistake." (source #61, p. 245)

On September 22, 1862, Lincoln announced that he would issue a formal emancipation of all slaves in any state of the Confederate States of America that did not return to

Union control by January 1, 1863. None did return and the actual order, signed and issued January 1, 1863, took effect except in locations where the Union had already mostly regained control. The Proclamation made abolition a central goal of the war (in addition to reunion), outraged white Southerners who envisioned a race war, angered some Northern Democrats, energized anti-slavery forces, and weakened forces in Europe that wanted to intervene to help the Confederacy. Total abolition of slavery was finalized by the Thirteenth Amendment which took effect in December 1865. (source #65)

7. John's wife was Laura Wilkinson Cleaver, my great-grandmother.

The 8th Reserve was at the Battles of Fredericksburg, Virginia, on December 12-15, 1862. They fought with greatest gallantry and experienced a heavier loss than on any previous field. Never before had it been subjected to so terrible an ordeal. James was wounded at Fredericksburg. (source #1, pp. 119-121; #2, pp. 757-761)

From January 20-24, 1863, the 8th Reserve was a part of the "Mud March." On February 8, 1863, the Reserves were ordered to the defenses of Washington, to rest and recruit. They remained on duty there and at Alexandria, Virginia, until the spring campaign in April 1864, at which time they were again ordered to the front. (source #36; #1, p. 122; #2, p. 762)

The letters James wrote from July 5, 1863, to March 28, 1864, were all written during this period of time.

THE LETTERS

———◦((◦))◦———

1863

Ward in the Carver General Hospital, Washington, D. C.
Courtesy of National Archives, photo no. 111-B-173

The following letter was written two days after the Battle at Gettysburg (July 1-3, 1863).

CARVER HOSPITAL[1]
JULY 5TH, 1863

Dear Father,

Your very kind and ever welcome letter came to hand day before yesterday. Since it was written, quite a change has taken place in affairs in Pennsylvania. Then the enemy seemed to be doing as they pleased and were quite jubilant over their apparent success, but now they have been beaten and discomfited and would gladly be back on their own accursed soil. They find that freedom's rain [sic] is death to traitors. I felt somewhat fearful when Hooker[2] was removed that all was not going right but his successor [George Meade] is an excellent man and I know from personal observations that there are no braver than he. You know he was at one time our Brigadier and afterward our Division Commander. And I <u>trust</u> that with the blessing of God he may lead our Army on to such a victory as it has never before accomplished. But I am sorry indeed that Gen. Reynolds has fallen. There was no officer in the Reserve or in the Army so universally loved and admired by our Division. He was certainly an officer of which Pennsylvania may well be proud of and one whose loss the country will feel, but alas such is war the bravest and best must fall and oh what an awful slaughter of human life has again taken place and how many cripples have been made within the past week.[3] How many fathers', mothers', sisters' and brothers' hearts are now and will continue to bleed for loved ones who "have for their country fallen."

I often think of this and it makes my heart sorrowful even while rejoicing for the success of our arms and at such times I grow impatient and restless. I long to be with my comrades and share with them their danger and toil and if they fall help to avenge their death but alas I cannot go.

The 4th was indeed a gala day to us at Carver and contrasted strangely with my last 4th of July. Then I was among men who loathed the name of freedom and abhorred the day which made us a nation and a free people. This year I spent it among a free people, among men who <u>love</u> the hallowed name of freedom, among men who are willing if needs be to die that our free institutions may be perpetuated to our sons and daughters of coming ages. Then I was confined in Richmond covered and surrounded by vermin and filth. Then I was a slave in body but not in spirit.

This year I was free in both and by thinking of [the] difference in my condition and the difference between the condition of the peoples of North and South was made to rejoice more than ever at the honor of being numbered among the soldiers of America.

But enough. We spent the day very pleasantly. An excellent dinner was prepared for us. An abundance of everything that our numerous and various appetites could crave being set before us and I think we did them justice. In the afternoon we were invited to Columbia College Hospital where we were entertained until evening with the enclosed program of exercises [missing from the letters], minus the band, but in its place we had a speech from the brother of Harper's Ferry John Brown.⁴ At 7 ½ o'clock we returned to our own hospital where we enjoyed a portion of the night in witnessing a display of fire works.

My health continues good for the past few days. We have been very busy making out Muster Rolls. I have not been in the city for some time and have not heard from my petition and do not know if it was accepted so I am not yet a Free Mason.⁵

It is now nearly breakfast time and I must close with love to all.

Your Very Affectionate Son,

James

AUTHOR'S NOTES

1. Carver General Hospital was located on Meridian Hill in the District of Columbia. It was near Columbia College General Hospital in wooden barracks that were formerly the Carver Barracks for the 102nd New York Volunteers. This hospital opened in April 1862 and closed in August 1865, sending its patients to Stanton General Hospital in July. (source #40)

2. Joseph Hooker (1814–1879) was a hard-drinking, egotistical general who may well have earned the nickname "Fighting Joe" for his contentious nature both on and off the battlefield. Battles such as the Seven Days' Fight and Yorktown demonstrated his leadership abilities, but the battle against General Lee at The Wilderness proved to be his undoing. Relieved of his duty, he was transferred to various locations in the Midwest that were not involved in active fighting. (source #46)

3. The Battle of Gettysburg is described as the war's turning point. Union Maj. Gen. Meade's Army of the Potomac

defeated attacks by Confederate Gen. Lee's Army of Northern Virginia. The battle with the largest number of casualties in the Civil War was also one of the bloodiest battles of the war. Of the 82,289 Union soldiers engaged, the number lost was 23,049. The Confederate Army engaged 75,000 and their casualties were 28,063. (source #45; #63) See the Appendix for more information on Civil War casualties.

4. John Brown (1800–1859) grew up in Ohio where he was taught by his parents to revere the Bible and hate slavery. In his adult years he became a militant abolitionist and a "conductor" on the Underground Railroad, and organized a self-protection league for free blacks and fugitive slaves. He had grandiose plans to free slaves throughout the South. With moral and financial support from prominent New England abolitionists, he and a small group of men began raiding southern plantations. On October 16, 1859, Brown and his men planned to raid the government armory and arsenal at Harper's Ferry. At the arrival of bands of militia and a company of U. S. Marines under Robert E. Lee, the raiders were trapped inside the fire-engine house. On the 18th, the building was stormed, which resulted in the death of ten of Brown's men and the capture of seven, Brown among them. After a sensational trial, he was found guilty and was hanged in Charlestown. Because of the stately manner in which he

conducted himself during the trial and on the gallows, he became a martyr in parts of the North. (source #9)

"I believe that to interfere, as I have done, in the behalf of God's despised poor is not wrong but right. Now, if it is deemed necessary that I should forfeit my life for the furtherance of the ends of justice, and mingle my blood further with the blood of my children and with the blood of millions in this slave country whose rights are disregarded by wicked, cruel, and unjust enactments, I say, let it be done."—Court statement, November 1, 1859. Brown said these words after being sentenced to death for his raid of the U. S. Armory. (source #61, p. 33)

5. Freemasonry is a fraternal organization that arose from obscure origins in the late 16th to early 17th century. Freemasonry now exists in various forms all over the world, with a membership estimated at around six million, including just under two million in the United States. After the American Revolution, independent U. S. Grand Lodges formed themselves within each state. George Washington was a member of a Virginian lodge. The fraternity is widely involved in charity and community service activities. There are thousands of philanthropic organizations around the world created by Freemasons, such as the Shriners Hospitals for Children. (source #47)

CARVER HOSPITAL
JULY 18, 1863

Dear Father,

I was glad to have the young Lieutenant from Mifflinburg call to see me for it is pleasant to see one who we know has but recently held intercourse with our kind beloved friends even though that person has hitherto been a stranger to us.

I thank him for taking so much trouble to come to see me which in his situation was no easy task for he seemed to be quite feeble and could not walk from the [train] cars to the hospital, but of this he has doubtless told you before now.

I had been in the habit for sometime of going in the evening to a creek to bathe and found him on that evening awaiting my return. Since then I have not been to bathe as the weather has been chilly and damp and I have taken a cold which has settled in my head and makes me feel uncomfortable. I am not sick from it but feel disagreeable as persons generally do when they have colds. I am still in the office and enjoy myself very well. I have not been to the City but twice for more than a month and then only a little while in the evening. I have not seen either Mathews or Lockies in the meantime. None of them have ever been to see me at the hospital although the last time I saw them they promised to do so.

I suppose the excitement consequent upon the invasion of Lee[1] and his defeat has died away with you, and Pennsylvania is again surrounded with a peaceful atmosphere.[2] New York City has been in an awful state.[3] The mob for some days seem[s] to have held undisputed control of the city, but thank heaven they have been checked and brought into subjection. The mob seem[s] to have been actuated almost entirely by a spirit for plunder and destruction and although certain parties would have us believe that it was caused by obnoxious points in the conscription bill, it is very plain that the draft had but very little if anything to do with it. But one thing is pretty certain, it was instigated by politicians opposed to the war for political ends but has recoiled upon their own heads and has killed the so-called Peace Democrat's party in New York, for every man with a spark of patriotism in his soul must look with horror and disgust upon such proceedings and the party that would encourage them.

I do not think we need fear such a thing occurring in Pennsylvania while Gov. Curtin holds the reins of State.[4]

The news from all our armies continues of the most cheering nature and the prospects now look brighter than ever before for a speedy termination to the war. Oh! that heaven may continue to bless our cause and soon restore us to peace, happiness, and prosperity as in days gone by.

Our regiment and one other of the Div. was left at Alexandria for provost and guard duty. Consequently [we] were not in the fight. I am glad of this for I could not very well have borne the idea of the regiment being there and I not with them.

Enclosed I send some of Mrs. Lincoln's hair taken from her head in this hospital. I want Lizzie to untangle it and put it on the hair tree if she can. The way it came to be cut off was in this wise.[5] As the President's Servant was conveying Mrs. Lincoln to their residence from Washington in a carriage, the horse ran away and threw her out, cutting her head against a stone. And as it occurred near here, she was conveyed into Dr. Judson's office where the hair was removed to have the wound dressed and of course a number of us being a little romantic eagerly seized a lock of this distinguished woman's hair.

I believe I know of nothing important to write about and must close and go to church.

With much love to Lizzie, Mother, and Mollie, I am

Your Very Affectionate Son,

James

Author's Notes

1. Robert Edward Lee (1807-1870) graduated second in his class from West Point in 1829. Upon graduation he was posted to the engineers working on projects in Georgia, Virginia, and New York. After his involvement with John Brown's Harper's Ferry Raid, he served in Texas until he was summoned to Washington in 1861 by Winfield Scott who tried to retain Lee in the U. S. service. The Virginian rejected the command of the Union's field forces on the day after Virginia seceded. As a Confederate brigadier general, and later full general, he was in charge of supervising all Southern forces in Virginia. Lee succeeded in keeping the Union forces in Virginia at bay for almost three years. After the war, he devoted the rest of his life to setting an example of conduct for thousands of ex-Confederates. He assumed the presidency of Washington College (now Washington and Lee University) in Lexington, Virginia. (source #9)

2. This is a reference to the Battle of Gettysburg.

3. The New York City Draft Riots raged during July 11–13, 1863. This was just four months after Abraham Lincoln

issued the Enrollment Act of Conscription (March 3). This act called for the enrollment of all able-bodied men. It carefully identified the men who were exempt such as the only sons of widows. However, Section 13 outraged much of the population as it allowed for the payment of a "commutation fee" whereby people could buy their way out of the draft lottery. By this time photographs of the battlefields and long casualty lists were being reported regularly in the newspapers. The idea that three hundred dollars could release a man from serving was met with resistance. Demonstrations took place in many Northern cities, but they were more violent and more publicized in New York, where Lincoln was despised by the hard-line members of the Democratic Party. During the four days of rioting in New York City, many attacks were aimed at black citizens, some of whom had recently replaced striking Irish longshoremen. Several beatings and lynchings occurred and a black church and orphanage were burned. More than $1.5 million in damage occurred. The number killed or wounded is estimated between two dozen and one hundred. In the end, the draft raised about 150,000 troops—just one fifth of the Union force. (source #37)

4. Governor Andrew Gregg Curtin (1817–1894) served the State of Pennsylvania from 1861–1867 during the dark years of the Civil War. He was credited with rallying support for President Lincoln and helping Pennsylvania play a key role

in the Union cause. He supported taxes to finance the war and coordinated recruiting measures. More military units for the war were organized in Harrisburg than in any other Northern recruiting point. This took place on an eighty-acre property named after the governor, Camp Curtin. During his second term he guided key efforts for the war through supplies, transport, support personnel, and the care of the troops in the field, as well as establishing a system of state schools for war orphans after the war. For these efforts he was known as "The Soldier's Friend."

After office he led reform fractions of the Republican Party. After losing a bid for the U. S. Senate to Simon Cameron, President Grant appointed Curtin as minister to Russia. Curtin later served as a Pennsylvania delegate to the Constitutional Convention of 1872–1873. His final political service was from 1881–1887 during which time he served three terms as a Democratic congressman.

Upon his death, Curtin was honored as a statesman and hero, and thousands paid their respects. Escorted by military troops who remembered his crucial role in the Civil War, he was laid to rest in Union Cemetery in his hometown of Bellefonte. (source #34, People, "Governors of Pennsylvania")

5. Wise, meaning "way or manner" (source #6)

CARVER HOSPITAL
AUGUST 11, 1863

Dear Father,

As [the] lieutenant from Union County is here and thinks of returning home, I will embrace this opportunity of hastily penning a few lines and sending them by him. My health is and has been good, but the weather is so very hot that all we can do is to sit and sweat. My time is now almost entirely occupied with duties in the office, so that I have but little time for anything else. I was, however, in the city a little while on Sunday afternoon at Mr. Lockie's and endeavored to learn a little in the first degree of masonry. I wish I had more time to devote to it.

I think I will soon go to my regiment had the weather not have been so warm. I think I should have gone this week.

I was in the city on last Saturday. Mrs. Williams, Eliza, and Samuel were there and spent a very pleasant day. They were on a week's visit to Alexandria to see Harvey.

I do not like to ask for money, but as I am at present five dollars in debt. If you have it to spare, I should be grateful for it. I do not like to leave here in debt.

I have not much time now, but will write again in a few days.

Your Very Affect[ionate] Son,

Jamie

Carver USG Hospital
Washington, D. C.
August 16, 1863

Dear Father,

Your kind letter enclosing $20.00 came to hand yesterday. It was more than I need at present unless I take to 2&3 degrees in masonry which I intend doing if I remain in the city long enough and I have now a great mind to do so. When I made up my mind to go back to the company, the prospects looked bright for a commission. But the Lieutenants told me that the Regiment was to be filled up with drafted men and had this been the case appointments would be made immediately. But since then I learn that there has no order been issued to fill up our Division and our numbers are now too small to allow 3 commissioned officers to a company and as we now have two, my prospects again look gloomy. I am sure, however, that both officers and all the company would do all in their power for me, but I think I shall now be governed by circumstances. I told the men when I was there on a visit that I intended shortly going back to stay with them and they may think it strange if I do not go. But I am sure they will not censure me for they all said if I came back I ought to receive a commission and when they learn how matters stand I think they say I do right. If I do go I do not expect to be able to stand a march. Dr. Judson tells me I never will and at present I know I can't, for my leg gives out in walking a short distance and as to marching with a knapsack and heavy load, I could not hope to be able to stand it.

If I was at the Regiment I should not spend so much money. Here our rations are very poor. Frequently I cannot eat them and crave something better, and of course if I get it I have to buy it and pay dear for it. My clothing also costs a great deal more here than in the Regiment, that is, I have to dress better. I intend, however, to spend less than I have been doing whether I stay or not. I sometimes go to Mr. Lockie's and get a good meal, but I am a little backward about sponging too much, although they are very kind and always tell me to come as often as I can. They always ask me when I heard from home and how all are.

I am glad you had such a pleasant trip to Jerseytown. There are some persons there I should like much to see. But there are many I would rather not meet. What do the people there think of our prospects now? I suppose the Union people are not so despondent as they were through the winter. And the traitors do not croak so much. I expect the war to be virtually ended before my term of service expires.[1] If Charlestown falls, which is almost a certainty, it will carry with it such a moral influence as will go far toward ending the struggle.

Let us hope that God will continue to favor us and increase the light, which is beginning to break through dark clouds that have so long been hanging over us. I often think that we ought to be much more grateful to Him, for He has done a great deal for us. Our condition has been and is vastly better than our enemies and if we have suffered greatly what must they have done.

I received a letter from John day before yesterday. He seems to be getting along pleasantly and continues to like his circuit. He expects Lizzie to visit them about the 25th of this month. It is now getting late in the evening and I must close with love to all.

Your Very Affectionate Son,

James

Author's Note

1. James's three-year term of service expired in May of 1864. Confederate resistance ended after General Lee surrendered to General Grant at Appomattox Court House on April 9, 1865.

    In the early hours of April 9, 1865, Lee was told by a staff officer that posterity would not understand why he did not escape. Lee relied, "Yes, yes, [posterity] will not understand our situation; but that is not the question. The question is, whether it is right; and if it is right, I take the responsibility." —Quoted by Edward Lee Childe in *Life and Campaigns of General Lee*, 1875. (source #61, p. 207)

    "We have fought this fight as long as, and as well as, we know how. We have been defeated. For us, as a Christian people, there is now but one course to pursue. We must accept the situation. These men must go home and plant a crop, and we must proceed to build up our country on a new basis." Quoted by Charles Francis Adams in *Lee at Appomattox*, 1902. On the morning Lee surrendered, he was turning down a suggestion by Brigadier General Edward P. Alexander to disperse the troops to fight on in smaller groups. (source #61, p. 207)

Upon his release from Carver Hospital, James rejoined his unit in the area of Alexandria, Virginia, where the 8th Reserve had been defending Washington, D. C., since February of 1863.

NEAR ALEXANDRIA, VA
DECEMBER 16, 1863

Dear Father,

Yours of the 9th came duly to hand and was received and was read with much pleasure. I am really glad to know that your health continues, and that the Lord is blessing your labors so abundantly in crowning you with success in the work He has given you to do. I hope and pray He may continue to preserve your health and strength for many years to come. This is constantly a source of great anxiety to me, and I am all the time more or less uneasy lest you may be sick. Yet thank God He has thus far been very merciful and kind to us and we ought certainly be willing to trust Him for all that is to come.

I am happy to say I am very comfortably circumstanced, very much more so than the Army in the field. We have certainly been very fortunate in being permitted to remain here so long and we will now most probably stay all winter, but when the spring campaign opens we will in all probability have to rejoin the army, and I don't know whether I would not rather do so, for soldiers on duty around cities far from danger are not likely to win a very enviable name among men who are fighting in the field. Tis time we must do just as the authorities say, having no will in the matter ourselves yet this is not generally taken into consideration.

We have a great deal of duty to do here—more than we would in the field, yet we have far more comfortable quarters and are in no more danger than we would be in the common avocations of life. Our barracks are now nearly finished. Two of the companies have already moved into them. We expect to move into ours on Thursday. The weather continues very fine. Sunday and yesterday were more like spring days than the middle of December. Sunday was [the] quarterly meeting in the M. E. church, but I was on duty that day and could not attend although I should have liked very much to have done so.

You ask me why it is that Meade's Army[1] meets with so little success compared with our Western Armies. The reason I think is that these armies (rebel and Union in Virginia) are so nearly equal that when either has the advantage in position it is impossible for the other to reroute it. It should be borne in mind that the flower of the rebel army is here in Va. to protect their capital, which must be done, whether they lose territories in other sections or not. For as the lines of the Confederacy now are, let Richmond fall and the rebellion is crushed.

From all that I can learn, I think Meade would have been very culpable before God and man to have dashed his army on the strongholds in which he found the enemy enclosed and thus have caused an immense slaughter with but slight hope of success. I send enclosed an article from the Chronicle [missing from the lettrs], which please read and preserve and tell me then if you do not think the General did right.

I still feel confident that next spring will end the war and that there will be very little fighting after our term expires. Remember me in love to Mother and Mollie.

Your Very Affect[ionate] Son,

Jamie

Author's Note

1. George Meade (1815–1872) In the first summer of the war, Meade was assigned to the division of Pennsylvania Reserves. After training and service near Washington, his command joined the Army of the Potomac on the Peninsula. During the Seven Days' Fight, he fought at Beaver Dam and Gaines' Mill before being wounded at Glendale June 30, 1862. After recovering, he led his brigade at 2nd Bull Run and the division of South Mountain and Antietam. With the invasion of Pennsylvania, he was chosen to relieve Joseph Hooker in army command only three days before Gettysburg. He masterfully shifted his troops from one threatened sector to another. He received the thanks of Congress and appointment as a brigadier in the regulars. However, he was soon criticized for allowing Lee to escape to Virginia without another battle. At Grant's request, he was advanced to major general in the regular army. He served in the Appomattox Campaign, but felt slighted by the reports which seemed to give all the credit to Grant and Sheridan. He mustered out of the volunteer service, and continued in the regular army, performing Reconstruction duty in the South. (source #9)

Main Street, Looking east, Everett, PA

Courtesy of Barbara Miller

The Letters

―――・((●))・―――

1864

Camp Near Alexandria, Va
January 28, 1864

Dear Father,

I beg you will pardon my seeming negligence in not writing you several days ago. I know you get uneasy unless you hear from me frequently and it is my desire to write every few days. Yet I often put it off without knowing myself the reason unless it is laziness. I have not, however, been very well for the past two weeks, being troubled with the diarrhea and a cough on account of which I have been relieved of duty on the Railroad and am again with the company and hope soon to be well again.

I came back day before yesterday and yesterday morning I received yours of the 23rd. I am glad to hear that your health is good and that Mother and Mollie have recovered from the mumps. I received a letter from John a few days ago. He's again able to be out on the circuit.[1]

We have had here some of the most delightful weather during the past week that I ever saw. It has been more like our northern spring than January. A day or two before I came from Cameron

Run several of us went fishing and caught 2 nice strings of pike. I had come to like it very much there. We had but little to do and having no boss over us it seemed much more independent than it does in camp. And I was sorry I asked to be relieved, but there being no doctor there I found my condition rendered it necessary. I was afraid that if I did not get the diarrhea checked it would become chronic. I am not bad and feel confident that with the blessing of Providence I shall soon be entirely well.

More of our men continue to join Veteran Corps.[2] Twelve have now re-enlisted, among them J. R. Callahan. They get four hundred dollars bounty and a furlough of 30 days. Five of our men are now on furlough. To-day the Captain has gone to Washington to enlist John Malone, brother to the Malone who died at Antietam. Recruiting officers have been sent out from the Regiment to go to the state and enlist men. John Tobias went from our company. Our squad has been away on that service since last summer, T. A. Taylor among them. We have now but 4 or 5 men with the rest being on permanent posts along the R Road picket, etc.

We have prayer meetings in our barracks once a week. Last night the meeting was very good although there were but few present.

The 5th Regiment are now encamped near us. They have come in for the purpose of guarding trains out to the Army. There is a rumor here that the whole division are [sic] coming here for duty. If this be correct, we will in all probability remain here until spring and be discharged in May. The 3rd and 4th Regiments are now doing duty at Martinsburg, Va., and not at Harper's Ferry as I told you in my last.

We are now all anxiously awaiting the arrival of the Pay Master. He was to have been here a week ago, but was disappointed in getting his money. He will likely be here about the first of next week.

There is a committee appointed and now sitting in Alexandria to examine such officers as Colonels of Regiments may wish. Some of our officers may be dismissed. I do not know whether I will be ordered before it or not. I think I can pass if I am.

It has been nearly two months since I was at Washington. I think I shall go over soon. Linn, Williams, and Callahan wish to be remembered. I believe I have now told you about all the news and with love to all will close.

Your Very Affectionate Son,

James

Author's Notes

Company F soldiers: (source #1, p. 122; #2, pp. 774-775; #54; #55)

John S. Malone, Private, recruited 1/28/61; transferred to 191st Regiment P. V., Company G, 5/15/64; captured, died in prison at Salisbury, NC, 10/24/64

William Malone, Private, mustered in 6/19/61; died of disease at Smoketown Hospital, MD, 10/24/62

John Tobias, Corporal, mustered in 6/19/61; promoted from Private to Corp.; absent on recruiting service since 1/21/64; mustered out with company 5/26/64

1. James's brother John, being a Methodist minister, made the rounds of churches in the area.

2. A possible reference to the Veteran Reserve Corps (originally the Invalid Corps), which was a military reserve organization created within the Union Army during the American Civil War to allow partially disabled or otherwise infirmed soldiers (or former soldiers) to perform light duty, freeing able-bodied soldiers to serve on the front lines. (source #41)

Near Alexandria, Va
February 14, 1864

Dear Father,

Yours of the 11th is at hand this morning. I am glad to hear from you always and to know that you are in [good] health and that the Lord blesses your labors. I am however sorry that there is likely to be a deficiency in your pay, for I know if you get all that is promised it will not be more than enough to live on, especially as everything is now so high. We have not been paid yet and will not probably be until 4 months is up. I should like very much indeed to attend conference this spring. The program would suit me exactly to go to conference at Altoona where I would doubtless meet many of my old Clearfield friends, afterwards go to Bedford Co., see our friends, and return to the army. I have no doubt as you say, the return of the Veteran Volunteers caused quite a lively and pleasant time in your town. The number of old soldiers who are re-enlisting does not look as though our armies are demoralized or tired of the war in the sense that Jerseytown used to preach it. We have 11 veterans in the company and 6 or 7 more will probably join the coming week. This will make about half of all belonging to the camp. It requires 2/3 to keep up the organization and allow us to go home in a body. This we can't get as some of our men are absent at hospitals and several that are with us are physically disqualified. Hence you see we would have to get every able man at least. I have heard a number of men say they would re-enlist if they could get into some other army. They seem tired of Virginia.

This is Sunday evening and the men have just returned from church. I have not been out to-day. I still have a cough and my bowels continue irregular. I think I will now try the effect of the recipes. I will now close bidding you all good night.

Your Very Affectionate Son,

James

are reinlisting does not look as though our
armies are demoralized or tired of the war
in the sense that Jersey town used to preach it.
We have 11 Veterans in the Company and 6 or 7 more
will probably join the coming week this will
make about one half of all belonging to the Comp.
It requires ⅔ to keep up the organization to
allow us to go home in a body this we cant
get as some of our men are absent at Hospital.
and several that are with us are physically
disqualified. hence you see we would have
to get every able man at least. I have heard
a number of the men say they would reinlist
if they could get into some other army. they
seem tired of Virginia.
This is Sunday evening and the men have
just returned from Church. I have not
been out to-day. I still have a cough and
my bowels continue irregular. I think
I will now try the effect of the recipies.
I will now close bidding you all good
night—
      Your very affect Son
        James

The second page of James's February 14, 1864, letter

193

Near Alexandria, Va.
February 20, 1864

Dear Father,

I expect to get home about the 1st of next month either on furlough or having resigned. The surgeon in charge of the Regiment gave me a pretty thorough examination this evening and tells me that if I wish to preserve my health, I must get out of the service and not expose myself. He said he would give me a furlough, but that he does not think it would do me much good. Hence, rather than ruin my health entirely, I think I had better resign at once. He said I must not follow any sedentary or indoor employment, but try to get on a farm or something of that kind. I do not seem to be much worse than I was when I wrote you last and I hope by leaving the service and taking care of myself to get well again. I will not write more now. Please answer soon. Advise me and if I come home about the first of the month where shall I come to?[1]

With love to all,
I am Your Very Affect[ionate] Son,

James

AUTHOR'S NOTE

1. James's father, being a Methodist minister, could well have been assigned to a church in another town at the time.

From 1862 to 1863, Rev. Charles Cleaver served at the Jerseytown United Methodist Church in Millville, Pennsylvania. He was in Mifflinburg, Pennsylvania, from 1863 to 1865.

COMPANY F, 8TH PA. RESERVES
FEBRUARY 28, 1864

Dear Father,

Yours of the 24th came to hand yesterday and was an answer to mine of the 20th. Since you wrote this I suppose you have received another note from me informing you of the improvement in my health and consequent detention of my resignation.

I am happy to say I still improve and my resignation being yet in the hands of the surgeon. I may withdraw it and remain in the service till the Regiment's time is up. I shall be governed by the advice of the doctor, doing nothing however that I may think will injure my health. Yesterday he spoke rather more encouragingly and the weather being fine he wishes to see what effect light out-door exercise will have on me before pronouncing the word which is to determine whether I shall remain in the service or not.

This is Sunday evening and the men are all absent, leaving me alone in the quarters. Some of them have gone to church and the rest are down at the picket line. We have but 4 men who now stay in the barracks—2 sergeants, 1 corporal, and 1 man. The others are either detailed away or now absent on furlough. Two more of our men went to Washington today to re-enlist, making 13 in all. T. A. Taylor called to-day. He is here with recruits for the army and will go back in the morning. He is fat as ever. Frank Holsinger spent a night with us last week. He has been appointed a first-class Captain in a Negro Regiment and looks well.

I should have gone to church this evening but for a boil in my nose.

Frank Jordon is now in Washington as Penna State Agent. You can easily find him for reference to assist you to procure a pass here. With love to friends,

Your Affectionate Son,

Jamie

AUTHOR'S NOTES

Company F soldier: (source #1, p. 122; #2., p. 774; #50; #54)

Frank Holsinger, Private, mustered in 6/19/61; discharged 2/11/64, to accept promotion to Sergeant

The final page of James's March 28, 1864 letter
Note the "long S" in "blissfull" (circled)

Near Alexandria, Va
Monday, March 28th, 1864

Dear Father,

In accordance with my promise I find myself seated this evening to write you although I must confess news is rather meager as nothing has occurred of interest or importance since you left.

I got safely back to the company on Friday evening. When we left the boat it was raining quite fast and the Capt. hired a hack to bring us out to camp. I don't think my trip to Washington did me much good. My bowels were quite troublesome on Saturday and yesterday, but this afternoon they are much easier, about the same as when you were here.

I have rubbed my breast with the mixture and will do so again to-night. I am also using the soap and opium.[1]

Capt. went to Washington again this morning with six more Veterans and has not yet returned. Williams is staying with me and he is now sitting at the end of the stand reading the Bible. J. R. Callahan was in a few minutes ago, but has gone out.

Yesterday and to-day the weather has been fine and pleasant, but it has got cloudy this evening and looks as though we may have more rain.

Quite a number of the troops who have been garrisoning the Forts around here have been sent to the front. This must go rough with them for they, as heavy artillery, supposed they would stay. Veterans among them have been so summoned that some of the regiments have filled to 1,800 men. Of course, Forts are nice places to soldier in, but alas! Man's fondest hopes are suddenly crushed. Marching orders swept away their blissful dreams and from comfortable quarters and a life of ease they find themselves with knap-sack upon their backs trudging through mud and mire toward the front.

We cannot yet tell whether we will be ordered away. The men don't or won't think that we will be. Yet marching orders may come suddenly. I hope not, however, as I am not able to go along.

I will now close and with love to Mother and Mollie, I am

Your Very Affectionate Son,

Jamie

Author's Note

1. Opium was a commonly used treatment for boils, a potentially painful affliction. (source #49)

James and his fellow soldiers were not alone in demonstrating their devotion to the cause. Local businessmen and shopkeepers agreed to close all shops and businesses in the event the Confederate Army moved into the area, thus not only protecting their goods and services but also making them unavailable to the Confederates. They issued the following statement:

We the undersigned merchants and store keepers of Bloody Run in consideration of the invasion of the North and the threatening of our National capital by an armed force of Rebels do promise, agree and bind ourselves to close all our stores and places of business and sell no goods nor do any business nor anyone for us in the way of buying and selling goods until the said Rebel force is defeated and driven back and those of our no. [number] who volunteered for the insurgency and go to aid their country in this its hour of peril have returned. Excepting that the post office may be open during office hours to hand news out but no one to enter inside and for the full and true performance of the above named agreements we pledge our swords our sacred honor and our all.

Bloody Run
July 13th, 1864

J. M. Barndoller & Son
J B Williams & Bro
Jere (Jeremiah) Baughman
Wm Masters
J A Gump
Thos Richey

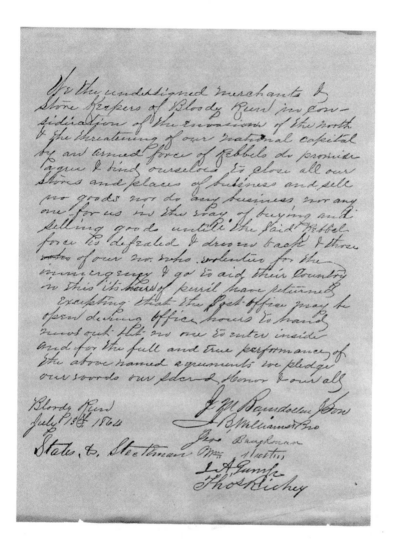

Original text of Businessmen's Agreement courtesy of Barbara Miller

Text on opposite page

THE FINAL WEEKS OF SERVICE FOR THE 8TH PENNSYLVANIA RESERVE

After concluding their duty in the Washington, D. C., area in April 1864, the 8th Reserve rejoined the Army of the Potomac. They moved forward with Gen. Grant into the wilderness. On May 4, they crossed the Rapidan and on the 5th were once more engaged with the enemy. It was here during the Battles of the Wilderness that James was wounded again. His regiment went on to fight Laurel Hill on May 8, the Battle at Spotsylvania on May 8-17, and the Assault at the Salient on May 12.

Their three years of service had now expired and on order from the War Department received on May 17, 1864, they were relieved of duty at the front. Recruits and re-enlisted veterans were transferred to the 191st Regiment. Those whose term had expired proceeded to Washington and then to Pittsburgh where on May 26, 1864, the remnants of the 8th Reserve were mustered out of service. Because James was in a hospital, he was absent when his comrades mustered out. (source #1, p. 122; #2, pp. 762-763)

APPENDIX

Cleaver, James   F - 8 Res   1 - 774

Enrolled 4-23-61   at Bedford Co.
M.I.   6-19-61 S.S. as 1st   at Camp Wilkins
          7-29-61 F.S.   Sergt. at Wash. D.C.
M.O.

Discharged

Age at enrollment 23   Complexion Light

Height   5'7½   Eyes   Blue

Hair   Light   Occup. Teacher

Residence-   Born - England

Remarks. (Prom. to 2nd Lt. 10-30-63- Bates)
     Wounded in action 5-10-64. Absent in Hosp.
          Ledger states age 36

James's enrollment card

JAMES CLEAVER

The following biographical information was gathered from his obituary, his military enrollment card, and the memoirs of his father.

James was born in England in 1838 and moved to America in 1844 with his family—his parents, the Rev. Charles and Elizabeth, and his siblings: John, age 11; James, age 7; Elizabeth (Lizzie), age 3; and Charles W., age 1. The family initially settled in Baltimore, Maryland. As a young adult James lived in Bedford County, Pennsylvania. He became a naturalized citizen.

Cleaver, James

Company F, 8th Reserve

Mustered in 6/19/61; at Camp Wilkins at the rank of Staff Sergeant; promoted to 1st Sergeant 7/29/61; promoted to 2nd Lieutenant 10/30/63; wounded in action 5/10/64; absent in hospital at muster out. (source #50)

James's final resting place

The following obituary of James Cleaver appeared in the *Bedford Gazette*, Bedford, Pennsylvania:

JAMES CLEAVER (6/26/1838 – 1/23/1911)

Mr. James Cleaver died at his home on North Richard Street, Bedford, Monday, Jan. 23 at the age of 72 years, 6 months and 27 days. He was born in England June 26, 1838, and was a son of Rev. Charles and Elizabeth (Dodd) Cleaver. He came to this country with his parents when quite young and located in Hopewell, where he engaged in the mercantile business. At the outbreak of the Civil War, he enlisted in Company F, 8th Pennsylvania Reserves, and was mustered into the service June 11,1861.[1] He was promoted 2nd Lieutenant, Oct. 30, 1863. He took part with his company in many battles during the Peninsula campaign, the Wilderness campaign and numerous other engagements. He was wounded four times, the last being at the Battle of Wilderness May 10, 1864. He was mustered out with his company in 1864, and returned to Hopewell, where he was married in the following year to Elizabeth Eichelberger, who died in 1882.

Mr. Cleaver was elected Register and Recorder of Bedford County in 1872, and held that office for six years. In 1885, he was married the second time to Miss Amanda Sansom, who survives him. [She died on January 5, 1923.] He was elected Prothonotary of Bedford County in 1896, and served six years.

Mr. Cleaver had been in failing health for about six years, during which time he suffered greatly. He was a member of the Bedford Methodist Episcopal church and took an active part in church work. He was Superintendent of the Sunday school for 20 years and was also class leader and steward. He was a member of the Odd Fellows at Hopewell, Bedford; Lodge No. 436 Order of the Knights of Pythias, Masons at Bedford, and the Grand Army of the Republic. Before his illness, he took an active part in the affairs of the county and of his hometown. In politics, he was a Republican and formerly took an active part in the affairs of the party. His honesty of conduct and integrity of character were never questioned, and for many years, he was looked upon as one of the best citizens of this community. Mr. Cleaver's only surviving relative, besides his wife, is one sister, Mrs. J. W. Gailey, of Bedford.

The funeral services will be held at the house at 10:30 o'clock this morning, conducted by Rev. W. V. Ganoe, assisted by Rev. George Laidy. Interment will be made in the Bedford Cemetery.

Author's Note

1. Depending on the source, Company F mustered in on June 11 or June 19, 1861. I have used the 19th throughout, because that was the date that appeared on their government enrollment cards.

REV. CHARLES CLEAVER (1815–1880)

(JAMES'S FATHER AND MY GREAT-GREAT-GRANDFATHER)

Source: The Minutes of the Ninety-Seventh Session of the Baltimore Annual Conference of the Methodist Episcopal Church held in M. E. Church, Martinsburg, W.V., March 9-15, 1881.

Rev. Charles Cleaver was born June 11, 1815, in Brackley, Northamptonshire, England. At the age of seven, he moved with his parents to Heath, Oxfordshire, where he spent his youth and early manhood. His parents were members of the Church of England and required young Charles to attend regularly the services of the Establishment. Charles was strongly attracted to the teachings of the Wesleyan ministry, and under their teachings, at the age of fifteen, was awakened to a sense that he was a sinner. His earnestness in seeking salvation of his soul, and subsequent union with the Wesleyan Church, aroused the opposition of his parents who abhorred all dissent. They put the steadfastness and principles of his faith to a severe test. Young Cleaver, however, was not wanting in the day of trial. Patiently enduring in the face of rebuke and suffering, Charles received the reward of his fidelity in seeing both his parents unite with the Communion which they had once despised, but in which he had found peace. At nineteen years of age, such was the esteem in which he was held that he was called to the local ministry of the Church and Circuit where he resided. He continued in that position until his removal to the United States on 1844.

Change of location did not work change in his religious principles—as it too often does—nor did it exhaust or terminate his duty to work in the Master's vineyard. Arriving in Baltimore, he sought out the people of God and was received as a member and local preacher by Caroline Street Station. He remained there until 1853 when he was recommended to the work of Itinerant Ministry, and entered upon its sacrifices and toils at the Session of the Baltimore Conference. From this time on, while strength endured, his life was given to the preaching of the Gospel. In the bounds of this and the East Baltimore Conference, through a period of twenty-three years, on extended and laborious charges, he did good, honest, earnest work for God. His fields of labor were as follows: Bald Eagle, Clearfield, New Washington, Schellburgh, Bedford, Jerseytown, Mifflinburg, Bloomingdale, Hereford, Bentley Springs, West Harford and Liberty Circuits.

Brother Cleaver apparently was a man of strong frame and vigorous physical powers, but vigorous and robust as he seemed, the time came at length, as it comes to all, when he must cease from active toil. In 1876, in consequence of failing health, his infirmities increasing upon him, he was compelled to take a super-numerary[1] relation and retired to the bounds of Hereford Circuit. Two years later, his infirmities increasing upon him, he was changed to superannuated[2] and continued in this relation until November 25, 1880, when at Hereford, Baltimore County, Md., his useful life on earth was terminated in prospect of a blessed and glorious immortality.

Rev. Cleaver is described by one who knew him as a faithful, earnest, and successful preacher of the gospel—loving and tender even to tearfulness in entreating sinners to seek salvation but firm and unswerving in his defense of what he regarded as the true and the right. He was not only generally useful and active in the duties of his calling, but very efficient in promoting revivals, visiting the sick, and looking after the poor and distressed of the flock. An anecdote related to him may serve to show his readiness to meet direct or indirect opposition, and exhibit the views he cherished as to the sources of authority ministerial. When residing in Mifflinburg and assisting in a series of Union Services, it devolved upon him to preach a sermon in a sister denomination on the Office of the Holy Spirit. This sermon he delivered with more than ordinary unction and power; so much so as visibly to affect the congregation he was addressing. Service being ended, the Pastor of the church, displeased at some of the positions taken, turned upon him and said, "By what authority do you preach such doctrine?" The immediate response was, "By authority of the Commander-in-Chief."

If Rev. Cleaver's active life was full of labor, his closing years were full of suffering. Retired to Hereford, his health gradually declined until twelve months prior to his death he was smitten with a stroke of paralysis. This so disabled him that he could not go about alone, but was compelled to use crutches and rely on the assistance of others. Another stroke six months later still further disabled him and gave increasing evidence that the end of his earthly sojourn was fast approaching. One of the especial [particular] afflictions of the last years of his life was his inability to attend upon the services of the sanctuary. Attentive as he had been to this duty, as to other duties of his calling, after his retirement from the active work of the ministry, he found himself in this last year cut off from this privilege. The last occasion, on which he is known to have attended upon Divine service, he sat in his carriage and weepingly listened to the word of God as it was expounded through the open windows. But in the midst of these depressing afflictions, Brother Cleaver was not without comfort. He "knew whom he had believed" and had a strong and abiding confidence in Him who has said, "I will never leave thee, nor forsake thee." His faith was firm, his hope steadfast and unshaken—and then he had the sympathy, the esteem, love, and attention of the many friends to whom he had ministered in the days of his laborious usefulness. We are told that Christian people from different parts of Hereford, Bentley Springs, and West Hartford Circuits came to see and ministered to him in his last illness, and with words of sympathy and deeds of love, smoothered his decline to the tomb. Thus it was, comforted by his friends, stayed and upheld by the hopes and joys of the Gospel, in his own home in Hereford, that Charles Cleaver, in the 66ᵗʰ year of his age, passed away from labor to reward.

Brother Cleaver was married three times and leaves a widow and three children to mourn his loss. One of his sons [John W. Cleaver] is now an active member of the Central Pennsylvania Conference.

We may write Charles Cleaver's epitaph in a single sentence: He was a faithful man and a good soldier of Jesus Christ.

Author's Notes

1. supernumerary refers to a disability leave. It was a category for ministers who were not old enough to be officially "retired" but who were unable for physical reasons to serve a church.(source #53)

2. superannuated means retired. (source #53)

REV. JOHN W. CLEAVER (1836–1884)
(JAMES'S BROTHER AND MY GREAT-GRANDFATHER)

Source: The minutes of the Seventeenth Session of the Central PA Annual Conference of the Methodist Episcopal Church, held in Huntington, Pennsylvania, March 12–17, 1885.[1]

Rev. John W. Cleaver was born in England on July 3, 1836. He came to America with his parents in 1844 and settled in Baltimore. His father, Charles W. Cleaver, who was a local preacher in England, joined the Jefferson Street Methodist Episcopal Church, Baltimore. At the age of 12, John was happily converted. He had presented himself at the altar of prayer during the day in the Sabbath School, and that night, while at his bed repeating the Lord's Prayer, when he came to the petition "Thy will be done," he felt that he was uttering the sincere desire of his heart, and immediately the burden was lifted, and he realized very clearly that God's spirit bore witness with his spirit that he was a child of God. He at once connected himself with the church and soon after became impressed that it was his duty to preach the gospel and began to prepare himself accordingly. In

1858 he was received on trial in the East Baltimore Annual Conference. His respective appointments were: 1858, Manor Hill; 1859, McConnellsburg; 1860, Westernport; 1861–62, Concord; 1863–64, Saxton; 1865–67, Newport; 1868–69, Half Moon; 1870–72, Milesburg; 1873–74, Williamsburg; 1875–76, Martinsburg; 1877–79, New Bloomfield; 1880–82, Mount Union. In 1883 he took a supernumerary relation and moved his family to Bedford, PA, where he died on December 3, 1884.

Brother Cleaver was an intense sufferer for several years. He consulted the most imminent physicians of Baltimore, Philadelphia, and other places, but all failed in giving permanent relief. Physicians differed as to the nature of his ailment. An autopsy revealed that a fatty degeneration and enlargement of the omentum and mesentery folds caused his death. The tumor and other abnormal fat weighed 130 pounds. And his burden he carried day after day with scarcely a murmur. He was confined to his bed only three weeks.

Brother Cleaver's social qualities and conversational powers were of a very high order. He possessed a vast source of general information and this combined with his cheerful disposition rendered him a most enjoyable companion. As a minister he was faithful, earnest, and successful. In every field in which he labored, sinners were converted, and believers strengthened and built upon the faith of the gospel. All through his illness he gave unmistakable evidence that it was well with him. A few weeks before his death, after a sinking spell, he remarked to his brother, "When the release comes, just the moment it comes, we will wonder that we wanted to live at all." His last words were, "Let me go home," then he sweetly fell asleep in Jesus. He was a kind husband and father, a good citizen, a true Christian, and an earnest, faithful, and successful minister.

He leaves behind his wife and five children. The funeral services, which were held in the Methodist Episcopal Church, Bedford, were conducted by the presiding elder, Rev. Richard Hinkle, assisted by Revs. George Bergstresser, A. D. Yocum, M. C. Piper, W. H. Stevens, and the pastor Rev. J. Harper Black. [One of his five children was my grandmother Anna Cleaver Ruff.]

Author's Note

1. The Central Pennsylvania Conference changed its name to the Susquehanna Conference in 2011. (source #53)

Thirty-Seventh Regiment, Eighth Reserve, Company F

Recruited in Bedford County, Pennsylvania

Names in bold are mentioned in the letters

Field and Staff Officers

John Eichelberger, Capt.

Eli Eichelberger, Capt.

Lewis B. Waltz, 1st Lt.

James Cleaver, 2nd Lt.

D. B. Armstrong, 1st Sgt.

John Paul, Serg't.

Jacob R. Callahan, Serg't.

John H. Williams, Serg't.

David Horton, Serg't.

Jacob B. Linn, Serg't.

Edmund H. White, Corp.

John Q. Leichty, Corp.

George Heffner, Corp.

Luther R. Piper, Corp.

John B. Tobias, Corp.

George Horton, Corp.

George Juda, Corp.

Wm. D. Ritchey, Corp.

Wm. H. Dasher, Corp.

Privates

Daniel Adams

George W. Amick

James Barber

John Barmond

Nathaniel Barmond

David Bollinger

Emanuel Bowser

James A. Bradley

George Brown

Levi Brumbaugh

James Capstick

John Carnell

Joseph S. Cook

Isaiah M. Davis

Franklin Dean

Christ Eastwright

Allison Edwards

Hiram Edwards

W. H. H. Eichelberger

Johnston Evans

Henry, Figart

Mark W. Foor

Samuel S. Foor

Wm. H. Foor

Aaron Foster

Robert Gamble

Christ C. Garlick

Alexander A. Garrett

James Gates

Abel Griffith

Michael Griffith

Wilson Grubb

David Headrick

Wm. Holdcraft

Frank Holsinger

Zopher P. Horton

Aaron Imes

Daniel Jordon

Wm. Harry Kay

George Leader

George Leichty

Joseph Leichty

Jacob Lines

Jacob Madara

Charles Malone

John S. Malone

PRIVATES (CONTINUED)

Wm. Malone

B. Manspeaker

David Manspeaker

Henry Marshall

David Martin

Joseph Maugle

Daniel McFarland

Joseph McFarland

Alexander H. McKee

Henry C. Penrod

John. B. Penrod, Jr.

John B. Penrod, Sr.

Lewis M. Piper

Joseph Ritchey

Conrad Robb

Oliver P. Ross

David Scutchall

Matthew P. Shaw

James Shields

Cornelius Shoaff

Henry Showalters

Simon Peter Showalters

Charles S. Smith

Thomas A. Taylor

George Tricker

Alexander Warsing

Wm. H. Whisel

John P. Williams

Alexander Young

Joel T. Young

(source #54)

8ᵀᴴ Pennsylvania Regiment Reserve Volunteers,
aka "the Thirty-seventh Pennsylvania Infantry"

FACT: "This distinguished regiment is included as one of William F. Fox's (c. 1889) top 300 Union Fighting Regiments."

SERVICE: Duty at Tennallytown, Md., August 2 to October 10, 1861, and at Camp Pierpont, near Langley, Va., until March, 1862. Skirmish at Great Falls, September 4, 1861. Advance on Manassas, Va., March 10-15, 1862. McDowell's advance on Falmouth, April 9-19. Duty at Fredericksburg until June. Moved to White House, June 9-11. Seven days before Richmond, June 25-July 1. Battles of Mechanicsville, June 26; Gaines' Mill, June 27; Charles City Cross Roads and Glendale, June 30; Malvern Hill, July 1. At Harrison's Landing until August 16. Movement to join Pope, August 16-26. Battles of Gainesville, August 28; Groveton, August 29; Bull Run, August 30. Maryland Campaign, September 6-24. Battles of South Mountain, Md., September 14; Antietam, September 16-17. Duty in Maryland until October 30. Movement to Falmouth, Va., October 30-November 19. Battles of Fredericksburg, Va., December 12-15. "Mud March," January 20-24, 1863. Ordered to Washington, D. C., February 6, and duty there and at Alexandria until April, 1864. Rapidan Campaign. Battles of the Wilderness, Va., May 5-7; Laurel Hill, May 8; Spotsylvania May 8-17. Assault on the Salient, May 12. Left the front May 17. Mustered out May 24 1864.

REGIMENT LOST: during service 5 Officers and 153 Enlisted men killed and mortally wounded and 68 Enlisted men by disease. Total 226.

(source #56)

PENNSYLVANIA'S ROLE
IN THE CIVIL WAR

Pennsylvania played a key role during the Civil War. Our industrial enterprise and natural resources were essential factors in the economic strength of the northern cause. Our railroad system, iron and steel industry, and agricultural wealth were vital to the war effort. The shipbuilders of Pennsylvania, led by the famous William Cramp Shipyards, contributed to the strength of the navy and merchant marine, including the Civil War's first submarine, *Alligator*, which was built at the Neafie & Levy Shipyard in 1861-1862. Thomas Scott, as Assistant Secretary of War, directed telegraph and railway services. Engineer Herman Haupt directed railroad movement of troops. Jay Cooke helped finance the Union cause, and Thaddeus Stevens was an important congressional leader.

Administration of military affairs during the war was directed by two Pennsylvanians: first by Simon Cameron, who resigned his seat in the U. S. Senate to become President Lincoln's first secretary of war; he was succeeded by Edwin M. Stanton of Pittsburgh.

A total of 427,286 Pennsylvanians served in the Union forces, which included 8,600 African-American volunteers. Looking at the grand total another way, 362,284 men responded to President Lincoln's call for volunteers for the Union Army and 25,000 Pennsylvania Militia men were called out in 1862, which accounts for 387,284 men, who served in 270 regiments and several detached companies of the Volunteer Army. Adding the 40,002 Pennsylvanians who enlisted in the United States Navy raises the total to 427,286.

Three days after the Confederates fired on Fort Sumter, Governor Andrew G. Curtin received a telegram from the secretary of war requesting that Pennsylvania provide two regiments who were wanted within three days. A sudden dash upon the capital was strongly threatened, and the city was entirely unprotected. Five militia companies were called up and sent immediately to Washington. These companies later became known as "The First Defenders" because they were the first military units to reach the Nation's capital.

In May 1861, the Assembly, at Governor Andrew G. Curtin's suggestion, created the Pennsylvania Reserve Corps of fifteen regiments enlisted for three years' service. They were mustered into the Army of the Potomac after the first Battle of Bull Run, and thousands of other Pennsylvanians followed them. Camp Curtin at Harrisburg was one of the major troop concentration centers of the war. Army leaders from Pennsylvania were numerous and able, including such outstanding officers as George B. McClellan, George G. Meade, John F. Reynolds, Winfield S. Hancock, Andrew A. Humphreys, John White Geary, David McMurtrie Gregg, and John F. Hartranft. In total, Pennsylvania had forty-eight general officers and fourteen commanders of armies and corps. One of these commanders was Galusha Pennypacker, of Chester County. He was the youngest general in either army during the war. Born June 1, 1844, he was only twenty when appointed Brevet Brigadier General U. S. Volunteers on January 15, 1865; Brigadier General U. S. Volunteers on February 18, 1865; and Brevet Major General U. S. Volunteers on March 13, 1865. He led the assault on Fort Fisher and was wounded seven times in eight months.

Private Richard Montgomery of the 155th Pennsylvania Volunteers was the last enlisted man killed in the fighting in Virginia. He was killed at Farmville, on the morning of April 9, 1865, shortly before General Robert E. Lee surrendered his Army of Northern Virginia to Lt. General Ulysses S. Grant.

From Erie, Pennsylvania, Oliver Wilcox Norton of the 83rd Pennsylvania Volunteers, a Brigade bugler, assisted General Daniel Butterfield in modifying the Infantry bugle call for Lights Out, thereby creating the hauntingly beautiful "Taps."

The 6th United States Colored Troops, recruited in Pennsylvania and trained at Camp William Penn, lost 62 percent of its men during an assault on New Market Heights near Richmond in 1864. Two of its members received the Medal of Honor for gallantry.

The 13th Pennsylvania Reserves, the "Bucktail Regiment," was recruited in the timbering counties of northwestern Pennsylvania. The Bucktails sported white-tailed-deer tails on their caps as a symbol of their skilled markmanship.

In the western theater, the 9th Pennsylvania Cavalry, assigned to the Army of the Cumberland, was the only eastern cavalry participating in Sherman's March to the Sea.

(source #48, #54)

CIVIL WAR FIRSTS

As the breeding ground for modern warfare, the Civil War has long been known for its "firsts." It has been credited with dozens like these:

- A workable machine gun
- A steel ship
- A successful submarine
- A "snorkel" breathing device
- A wide-ranging corps of press correspondents in battle areas
- American conscription
- American bread lines
- American president assassinated
- Aerial reconnaissance
- Antiaircraft fire
- Army ambulance corps
- Blackouts and camouflage under aerial observation
- Cigarette tax

- Commissioned American army chaplains
- Department of Justice (Confederate)
- Electrically exploded bombs and torpedoes
- Fixed ammunition
- Field trenches on a grand scale
- Flame throwers
- Hospital ships
- Ironclad navies
- Land-mine fields
- Legal voting for servicemen
- Long-range rifles for general use
- Medal of Honor

- Military telegraph
- Military railroads
- Naval torpedoes
- Negro U. S. Army officer (Major M. R. Delany)
- Organized medical and nursing corps
- Photography of battle
- Railroad artillery
- Repeating rifles
- Revolving gun turrets
- The bugle call, "Taps"
- The income tax

- The wigwag signal code in battle
- The periscope, for trench warfare
- Telescopic sights for rifles
- Tobacco tax
- U. S. Navy admiral
- U. S. Secret Service
- Withholding tax
- Wire entanglements
- Wide-scale use of anesthetics for wounded

(source #44)

CIVIL WAR CASUALTIES

The Civil War remains the deadliest war in American history, resulting in the deaths of 620,000 soldiers and an undetermined number of civilian casualties. Ten percent of all Northern males 20–45 years of age died, as did 30 percent of all Southern white males aged 18–40. These casualties exceed the nation's loss in all its other wars, from the Revolution through Vietnam.
(Source #45, #59)

The Union armies had from 2,500,000 to 2,700,000 men. Their losses, by the best estimates:

> Battle deaths: 110,070
> Disease, etc: 250,152
> Total: 360,222

The Confederate strength, known less accurately because of missing records, was from 740,000 to 1,250,000. Its estimated losses:

> Battle deaths: 94,000
> Disease, etc.: 164,000
> Total: 258,000

Some of the great bloodbaths of the war came as Grant drove on Richmond in the spring of 1864. Confederate casualties during this campaign were enormous, but the exact number is unknown. The Federal toll:

The Wilderness, May 5-7:	17,666
Spotsylvania, May 10 and 12:	10,920
Drewry's Bluff, May 12-16:	4,160
Cold Harbor, June 1-3:	12,000
Petersburg, June 15-30:	16,569

(source #45)

BIBLIOGRAPHY

#1   *History of Bedford, Somerset, and Fulton Counties*, Vol. R. Chicago: Waterman, Watkins & Company, 1884

#2   Samuel Bates, *History of Pennsylvania Volunteers 1851–1865*, Vol. I, Wilmington, NC: Broadfoot Publishing Company, 1993. This book is also available online: http://www.pacivilwar.com file: Bates

#3   John J. Matviya, Basic Training at Camp Wilkins and Camp Wright, http://www.9thpareserves.org/library09.htm

#4   *Bedford Gazette*, June 10, 1995, Everett Bicentennial

#5   http://wordsmith.org/words/chapfallen.html

#6   *Webster's New World Dictionary*, New York: Simon & Schuster, Inc., 1990

#7   http://www.batteryb.com/taps.html

#8   http://en.wikipedia.org/wiki/George_A._McCall

#9   http://www.civilwarhome.com/biograph.htm - Civil War Biographies

#10   www.civilwarhome.com/CMH1stmanassas.htm - Jackson

#11   http://www.civilwarhome.com/terms.htm - Civil War Potpourri, "Definitions of Civil War Terms"

#12   http://civilwarbluegrass.net/battles-campaigns/1862/620200.htm

#13   http://www.cr.nps.gov/hps/abpp/battles/va005.htm

#14   http://www.nps.gov/mana

#15   http://www.nps.gov/fosu

#16   http://www.tulane.edu/~latner/Anderson.html

#17   http://www.jarnaginco.com/raingear.htm

#18   http://www.civilwarhome.com/civilwarmedicineintro.htm - Civil War Medicine

#19   http://chronicles.dickinson.edu/encyclo/b/ed_butlersanalogy.html

#20   http://civilwartalk.com/forums/showthread.php?27984-Raising-the-black-flag&highlight=raise+the+black+flag

#21   http://en.wikipedia.org/wiki/John_Adams_Dix#Civil_War_service

#22   Frank Leslie, *Famous Leaders and Battle Scenes of the Civil War*. New York: Mrs. Frank Leslie, 1896

#23   http://en.wikipedia.org/wiki/Bsllston,_Arlington,_Virginia

#24   http://dmna.state.ny.us/historic/reghist/civil/infantry/65thInf/65thInfMain.htm#photos

#25   http://www.civilwarhome.com/records.htm - Civil War Battles

#26   http://civilwar.bluegrass.net/FamousUnits/pennsylvaniabuck-
        tails.html

#27   http://www.civilwarinteractive.com/recipeFLANNEL
        CAKES.htm

#28   http://www.civilwarhome.com/cottondiplomacy.htm - Civil War
        Potpourri, "Cotton King"

#29   http://en.wikipedia.org/wiki/Battle_of_Ball's_Bluff

#30   Battlehttp://en.wikipedia.org/wiki/Charles_Pomeroy_Stone

#31   http://www.civilwarhome.com/potpourr.htm - Civil War
        Potpourri, "Balloons with the Army of the Potomac"

#32   http://en.wikipedia.org/wiki/Pancho_Barnes

#33   http://www.civilwaracademy.com/horace-greeley.html

#34   Pennsylvania Historical and Museum Commission / history /
        Pennsylvania history / people   http://www.portal.state.pa.us/
        portal/server.pt?open=512&objID=4277&&PageID=443541&le
        vel=4&css=L4&mode=2

#35   http://www.civil-war-tribute.com/edwin-stanton-bio.htm

#36   http://www.pacivilwar.com/regiment/37th.html

#37   http://www.civilwarhome.com/potpourr.htm - Civil War
        Potpourri, "New York Riots"

#38   http://www.sonofthesouth.net – *Harper's Weekly*

#39   http://onlinedictionary.datasegment.com/word/grand+guard

#40   "Washington and Georgetown, D. C.," *Indexes to Field Records of Hospitals, 1821–1912*, Manuscript Record Group 94, National Archives

#41   http://en.wikipedia.org/wiki/Veteran_Reserve_Corps

#42   http://www.merriam-webster.com/dictionary/muster+roll

#43   http://en.wikipedia.org/wiki/James_H._Lane_(Senator)

#44   http://www.civilwarhome.com/civilwarfirsts.htm

#45   http://www.civilwarhome.com/casualties.htm

#46   http://www.civilwaracademy.com/joseph-hooker.html

#47   http://en.wikipedia.org/wiki/Freemasonry

#48   http://en.wikipedia.org/wiki/Taps

#49   http://www.civilwarhome.com/drugsshsp.htm

#50   for Civil War Enrollment Cards: http://www.digitalarchives.state.pa.us

#51   http://www.sullivanpress.com/Spencerian.htm

#52   http://www.6nc.org/about6nc/copperplate.html

#53   Milton Loyer, the Susquehanna Conference archivist

#54   http://www.pa-roots.com/pacw

#55   http://cairo.pop.psu.edu/cw

#56 http://www.mosocco.com/penna.html

#57 http://www.mdgorman.com/Prisons/Libby/libby_prison.htm

#58 *Bedford Gazette* article, "Hopewell Rifles Went to War in '61 When Lincoln Called," written around 1975 by Ned Frear – Now a retired journalist, he remembers that the 3-part series on the Hopewell Rifles was one of his first assignments. These articles were brought to my attention by Kay Leach at the Pioneer Library of the Bedford County Historical Society, bedfordhistory@embarqmail.com

#59 http://www.zampwiki.com/?t=American_Civil_War

#60 "From Bloody Run to Everett" A History of the Five Names of Everett, written by Jeffery S. Whetstone

#61 *The Oxford Dictionary of Civil War Quotes,* edited by John D. Wright, Oxford University Press, 2006

#62 http://en.wikipedia.org/wiki/Baltimore,_Maryland

#63 http://en.wikipedia.org/wiki/Battle_of_Gettysburg

#64 http://www.merriam-webster.com/dictionary/detached%20service

#65 http://en.wikipedia.org/wiki/Emancipation_Proclamation

#66 http://en.wikipedia.org/wiki/United_States_presidential_election,_1860

Milann Ruff Daugherty

ABOUT THE AUTHOR

Milann Daugherty grew up in Western Pennsylvania and graduated from Westminster College with a bachelor's degree in elementary education. Because her husband was in the Air Force, she taught in several locations including the Milton Hershey School in Hershey, Pennsylvania, and Okinawa, Japan, before settling down to raise their two children.

In 1991 Milann returned to teaching and taught for sixteen years at the New Castle Christian Academy in Pennsylvania. It was here that her interest in American history was ignited, for it was part of the fourth grade curriculum that she taught. As a result, she was primed for the extraordinary gift of the discovery of her great-great uncle's Civil War letters.

She is an active member of P.E.O. International (Philanthropic Educational Organization) and has served as president of the P.E.O. Pennsylvania State Chapter. She also keeps busy with hand bell ringing, knitting, and sewing.

In 2007 she and her husband moved to Ohio where he teaches at a state university, and they are able to be nearer their grown children and four grandchildren.

WA